AMERICA IN MINIATURES

A compilation of MODELS OF AMERICA'S PAST AND HOW TO MAKE THEM
and HISTORIC MODELS OF EARLY AMERICA

AMERICA IN MINIATURES

How to Make Models of Early American Houses, Furniture, and Vehicles

C . J . M A G I N L E Y

**Illustrated by Elizabeth D. McKee
and James MacDonald
Photographs by Joseph Moffa**

Harcourt Brace Jovanovich   New York and London

Library of Congress Cataloging in Publication Data

Maginley, C. J.
    America in miniatures.

    Compiled from the author's Models of America's past
and Historic models of early America.
    1. Models and modelmaking. 2. Miniature objects—
United States. I. Title.
TT154.M24   745.59′2   76-13002
ISBN 0-15-105587-4

First Edition

B C D E

CONTENTS

AUTHOR'S NOTE

By building a miniature model of some object used by our ancestors the builder will relive something of the past history of America. The models in this book are miniatures of things made by our forbears with their own hands and with crude tools.

By constructing a little cradle or an old meetinghouse the modelmaker will be made more aware of life as it was in our country in earlier times. He or she may come to appreciate more the contribution made by those rugged pioneers of yesteryear in laying the foundations for the America of today.

Making a model is also an excellent way to relax and create with the hands what is conceived by the mind. Many enjoyable hours can be spent building a miniature.

EDITOR'S NOTE

Some things never go out of fashion; they simply become more fashionable at times and less fashionable at other times. Since earliest records of human life, the making of miniatures has been part of the life of every known group. Tiny doll-like representations of human form and of everyday objects have been discovered in caves and graves in China, South America, Europe, and even the Arctic. People enjoy creating and displaying the small figures and objects that reflect the daily life around them. We are no different.

This year is the 200th birthday of our country, the United States of America. What was it like to live when our country was founded? What sort of furnishings, vehicles, and equipment did the early settlers use? We can relive, in a very pleasant way, the building of the first log cabin, and the fashioning of a hutch, a table, a bed, or a butter churn by making the objects in scale—in miniature.

This book has been compiled from two earlier books by C. J. Maginley. The suggested projects have been selected because they represent the basics of a small early American village and home. The original editions of C. J. Maginley's books, MODELS OF AMERICA'S PAST AND HOW TO MAKE THEM and HISTORIC MODELS OF EARLY AMERICA are still in print, and available through Harcourt Brace Jovanovich, Inc. This book includes some of the same material in a new format and with some new techniques.

We expect that in another 200 years, people will still be making miniatures; perhaps they will show buildings of today, in small replicas. They might act out exciting and important events, just as the making of miniatures allows us to relate to our past.

The making of miniatures is suitable for eight-year-olds and eighty-year-olds; for artists, designers, modelmakers, doll house keepers, and for fun and collecting. Small scraps of wood, bits of cloth, and tiny wires can be used to fashion entire scenes. Miniatures are fun and of historic importance; they will provide hours and hours of activity and pleasure for the maker and user. We hope you enjoy this newly issued book and that it makes your miniature-making very big.

GETTING READY

Tools

The author assumes that only hand tools may be available to the model builder. All of the models in this book can be made with the tools listed below.

Coping saw with fine blades
Hand drill
Drills which should include:
numbers 43, 44, 45, 52, 60, 70
and also ⅛, ³⁄₁₆, ¼

Small hammer
Vise
Files, flat, round, half-round
Chisel
Small pliers
Sharp knife
Try square
Wire cutters
Sandpaper, fine, medium
Emery boards
Single edge razor blades
"Tiny Tim" hack saw
Compass
Awl
Ruler

Materials—Wood

Soft woods such as pine or basswood are best for making most of the parts for the models. Plywood, available at hobby stores in different thicknesses, is good for making parts where there is any danger of splitting, such as the rims for the wheels. Maple or birch are good hard woods to use.

Balsa wood can be cut more easily than the pine or basswood but is very soft. However, when wood $\frac{1}{64}''$, $\frac{1}{32}''$, or $\frac{1}{16}''$ in thickness is needed, balsa wood is very good.

Small pieces of wood can often be obtained from the scrap pile at a cabinetmaker's shop, lumberyard, or woodworking plant. There are many "do-it-yourself" craftsmen with power tools who might also be a good source for small pieces of wood.

Materials—Miscellaneous

White glue
Rubber bands
Common pins
Round toothpicks
Flat toothpicks
Paper clips
Florist's wire
Applicator sticks
Transparent plastic—$\frac{1}{64}''$–$\frac{1}{32}''$ thick

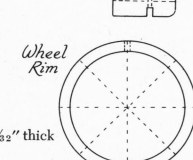

Cross Section of Hub

Wheel Rim

MAKING WHEELS

The Hub

Make the hub from a piece of $\frac{1}{2}''$ or $\frac{5}{8}''$ dowel. Cut a groove about $\frac{3}{32}''$ deep around the hub for the spokes to fit into. A saw cut can be made first and enlarged with a file. Make the groove before cutting the hub to the desired length. Drill a hole lengthwise through the center of the hub for the axle and another hole, the size of the spokes being used, through the hub in the opposite direction. This second hole should go through the hub where the groove was made. Taper one end of the hub with a file and sandpaper.

The Rim and Spokes

The best material to use for the rims of the wheels is 1/8", 3/16", or 1/4" plywood. Round toothpicks, applicator sticks, or 1/16" dowels can be used for the spokes.

When constructing a wheel, first draw a circle on the plywood with a compass. Draw an inner circle about 3/16" to 1/4" inside the first one. Before cutting out the disk, draw two or more diameters perpendicular to each other. These lines will be useful as guides when drilling the holes for the spokes. Saw out the disk and round off the edges with sandpaper. Divide the disk into eight or twelve equal parts, depending on the number of spokes to be used. Make a line on the circumference at the end of each radius. Then make a mark with an awl in the exact center of the circumference of the disk and drill holes for the spokes to a depth of 3/8" or so. Saw out the inner disk, leaving the rim of the wheel. Insert a piece of spoke material through the rim, the hole in the groove of the hub, and on through the rim on the other side. Center the hub on this spoke material. Insert other spokes through the remaining holes in the rim and into the groove, in which a little glue has been put. Cut off any protruding ends of spokes and finish with sandpaper.

INSTALLING WINDOWS

Windows can be purchased at a hobby store in a variety of kinds and sizes. Some windows are printed on plastic, while others are molded from plastic or made of lead. The latter types, with the frame and sill, can be set into the openings and give the model a very finished appearance. The ⅜″ by ⅝″ window openings in all of the buildings described in this book are the size of the lead windows. The model builder will have to make any necessary changes in the size of the openings to conform to windows of a different size that he may buy.

When making the openings for windows, cut them a little smaller than the dimensions of the window being used and finish to the correct size with a flat file. The windows used by the author have twelve panes of "six over six." It is also a good idea to glue the windows in place before assembling the building.

If the printed windows are used, they should be glued to the outside of the building over the opening and then a narrow frame of thin wood put around them.

Windows can be made by drawing lines to represent panes on fairly heavy plastic. Waxed paper can also be used and the panes outlined on it with a toothpick or pin. If waxed paper is used, it is best to fasten it to the inside of the building with tape and outline the panes afterward.

MAKING AND HANGING DOORS

1. Drill a hole, for a piece of paper clip or pin, through each door support ¹⁄₁₆″ from one end. The supports should be as long as the door is wide.

2. Drill a slightly larger hole in each end of the door about ¼″ in depth and also ¹⁄₁₆″ from one edge.

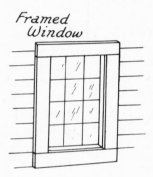

Framed Window

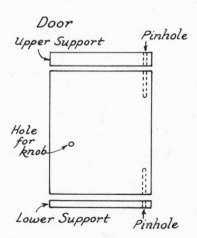

Door
Upper Support   Pinhole

Hole for knob

Lower Support   Pinhole

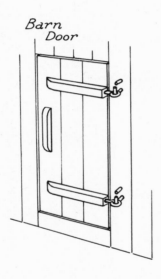

*Barn
Door*

*Hinge
Parts*

← ⅜˝ →

3. Drill a hole for the knob about ³⁄₁₆″ from the other edge and a little less than halfway up from the bottom of the door.

4. Glue the lower door support to the floor in front of the doorway.

5. Round off the corners of the edge of the door on the hinge side.

6. Insert a piece of pin or paper clip into the hole in the lower end of the door, letting it extend ¹⁄₁₆″ or a little less.

7. Set the door in position with the wire in the hole in the support.

8. Glue the upper support directly above the lower one and a trifle above the end of the door so that it will not bind. Be sure that the holes in the supports and the door are in a straight line.

9. Insert a piece of wire down through the hole in the upper support into the hole in the door.

10. If the door binds, remove it and round off the edge a little more.

THE BARN DOORS

The doors for the barn can be made from one piece of wood or narrower pieces can be glued together to obtain the width needed. Make the doors a trifle narrower than the width given so that they will open and close easily.

The hinges, made from ⅛″ by ⅛″ wood, should be ⅛″ shorter than the width of the door. Glue the hinges to the door ¼″ from either end with one end of the hinge even with the edge of the door. The other end of the hinge should be rounded off with sandpaper. Drill a hole, slightly smaller than the wire being used for the eyes, in the center of the ends of the hinge. Make the eyes as shown in the drawing and insert them into the holes. The best way to make the eye is to put a small nail, with the point up, in the vise and bend the wire around it. Cut off one end of the U-shaped wire and bend the short end remaining around the nail to form the eye. Glue the handles to the doors about midway between the top and bottom and $\frac{1}{8}$″ from the edges.

Set the doors temporarily in place and mark the location of the hangers. Drill holes for the hangers, which should be approximately $\frac{1}{16}$″ from the edge of the doorframe. The hangers should fit snugly in the holes. In order to prevent the doors from coming off the hangers, a hole can be drilled, slightly above one of the eyes, and a piece of wire inserted into the hole.

ROOFING THE BUILDINGS

When applying the roof boards, leave a little space between them and cover or box in the ends as follows:

Measure the distance from the peak of the roof to the end of a rafter. Glue a piece of wood ($\frac{1}{16}$″ x $\frac{1}{2}$″ for stone barn) by the measured length to the underside of the roof boards where they extend beyond the ends of the barn. The piece will also be against the end. Measure and glue a second piece to the other side of the roof. These pieces will extend about $\frac{1}{8}$″ beyond the ends of the roof boards. Glue strips $\frac{1}{16}$″ by $\frac{1}{8}$″ by the needed length, to the upper side of the first pieces where they extend beyond the ends of the roof boards. If the peak is a right angle, as the peak of the barn is, the pieces will not have to be cut at a 45-degree angle. The shorter piece will butt against the longer piece at the peak to form a right angle.

The pieces for the schoolhouse and meetinghouse must be cut at the same angle or slant as the roof. The 1/16″ by 1/8″ wood must be the same thickness as the roof boards.

The ends of the roof boards on some old barns were not boxed in. This step may be omitted.

APPLYING THE SHINGLES

Cut the shingles 1″ in length and in three or four different widths from 1/4″ to 1/2″. Use 1/64″ material if available; the thinner the shingles are, the better. Starting at the lower edge of the roof, apply the first row, allowing the ends to extend an 1/8″ or so at the lower edge of the roof. If 1/32″ material is being used, when the glue has set, sandpaper the upper ends to make them thinner before putting the next row on. An emery board is good for this purpose. Leave a little space or crack between each shingle and place them so that 1/2″ of each row is "exposed to the weather." Use shingles of varying widths so that the spaces or cracks between the shingles in one row are not in line with those in the preceding row.

It is a good plan to work first from one side of the roof and then the other to allow the glue to set. When near the peak, cut the shingles for the last rows to the length required so that they will meet from the two sides at the peak.

Glue a thin ridge board, as long as the building and 1/4″ to 3/8″ wide, depending on the size of the structure, to each side of the peak. One of these boards should overlap the edge of the other.

Roofs can also be made in two pieces, one overlapping the other at the peak. However, shingling the roof makes

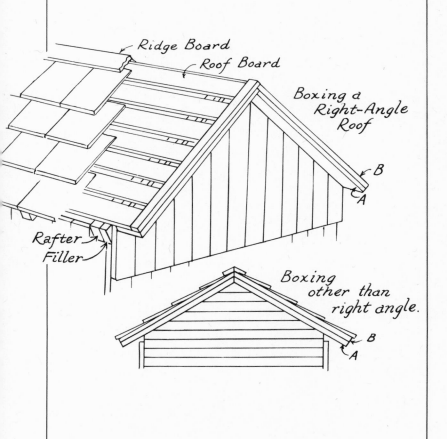

Ridge Board
Roof Board
Boxing a
Right-Angle
Roof
B
A
Rafter
Filler
Boxing
other than
right angle.
B
A

a much better-looking model and is recommended by the author.

SOME SUGGESTIONS

A well-known educator once said that everyone should be able to make something with his hands of which he can be proud. If the craftsman is to be proud of the model he has made, he must make sure that all parts are carefully sanded before they are assembled as well as afterwards. The care that is taken in sanding will determine whether the model is a finished one, of which he can be proud, or otherwise. Here are a few suggestions for sanding and some general points to bear in mind:

Sandpaper with the grain of the wood and not across it.

Make a sanding block by wrapping sandpaper around three sides of a block of wood.

Emery boards are very good for sanding small pieces.

Rub small pieces of wood on the sandpaper.

Use medium and then fine sandpaper.

Smooth all edges of the completed model with fine sandpaper.

Used power-sanding belts, cut into pieces, make very good material for sanding. A fine belt is best.

To sand concave surfaces, wrap a piece of sandpaper around a dowel that is a little smaller than the curve to be sanded.

When two like pieces are needed, such as for the ends of a desk, put them in the vise, after they have been sawed out, and finish with a file and sandpaper.

Throughout the book, *pc* stands for *piece*.

Use the try square when marking on wood to assure straight lines.

Wire can be made flat by pounding it with a hammer.

Read the instructions all the way through before starting to build a model.

The size of the drill to use will depend on the size of the wire being used and may be different from the drill suggested.

The modelmaker will have to make adjustments from time to time as the wood being used may be thinner or thicker than the dimensions given. He may also wish to use thicker material than that called for to make a sturdier model. The ends and rockers for the cradle, for example, might be made from ⅛″ stock instead of 1⁄16″ as in the book.

The modelmaker may want to leave one side of the roof only partly covered so as to be able to look inside the building.

When two pieces of wood are to be glued together, spread a thin layer of glue on one of the pieces. Do not use too much glue; a little is better than a lot. Press the pieces firmly together. Some parts can be held together with rubber bands or with weights until the glue has set. One of the white glues is excellent for making models, such as Elmer's glue.

FINISHING THE MODELS

The models, unless otherwise suggested, may be stained and then lacquered, shellacked or varnished. Or they may be left natural as the wood will color with age. If left natural, however, it is a good idea to apply two or three coats of a clear finish. Such finishes can be applied with a small brush, or they are available in spray cans at paint or hobby stores. If a weather-beaten appearance is desired for the buildings, stains may be used to get that effect.

THE HOUSE

A LOG CABIN

The log cabin is a true symbol of early America. These sturdy dwellings, usually built by community effort, were the first homes of the pioneers. The logs were notched at each end and were laid one on another so as to interlock at the ends. A roof or wooden slabs usually covered the cabin. Mud and sticks were used to fill in the cracks between the logs. The chimney was often made from small logs plastered with mud.

Materials

16 pc ⅜″ dowel 7″ long—sides
14 pc ⅜″ dowel 5″ long—ends
 2 pc ⅜″ dowel 3⅝″ long ⎤
 2 pc ⅜″ dowel 2¾″ long ⎥ gable ends
 2 pc ⅜″ dowel 2″ long ⎥
 2 pc ⅜″ dowel 1¼″ long ⎦
 7 pc ¼″ dowel 7″ long—roof rafters
 3 pc ¼″ dowel 5″ long—crossbeams
28 pc ⅟₃₂″ x ¾″ x 3″—roof slabs
 1 pc ⅟₃₂″ x ½″ x 7″—ridge board
 6 pc ⅛″ dowel 7¼″ long—roof slab binders
 1 pc soft wood ¾″ x 2½″ x 6″—chimney
    (Or ¼″ and ⅛″ dowel if chimney is made from logs)
 2 pc ⅟₁₆″ x ⅜″ x 1¾″—doorframe
 1 pc ⅛″ x 1⅛″ x 1¾″—door
 2 pc leather ⅟₁₆″ x ³⁄₁₆″ x ½″—hinges

Construction

1. File a notch with a round file
½″ in from each end of two of

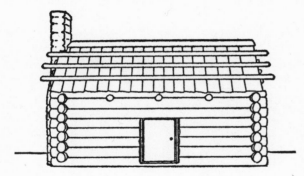

the 7″ logs, or make a notch with a knife. Make the notches about ⅛″ deep and about ⅜″ long.

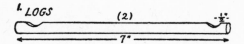

2. Then file similar notches in all of the 5″ logs and in twelve of the 7″ logs. Make, however, one notch on the upper side and one on the lower side of each of these logs. Lay the two 7″ logs, with one notch in them, on the workbench with the notch upward, and lay two of the 5″ logs across them so that the lower notch of the shorter log fits into the notch cut in the longer log. Peg or glue together to make a firm foundation. Continue in this way until the cabin is five logs high. Saw out openings for the door and the window. The door opening should be 1¼″ x 1¾″ or down through four logs and part way through the lower log. Make the window opening about ¾″ wide and down through two logs. Then continue laying the logs until the cabin is 7 logs high. Finish the sides of the cabin by making notches in the remaining two 7″ logs as shown. Make notches ½″ from the ends in one side of each of the three ¼″ dowels being used for crossbeams. Lay these crossbeams across the upper side logs so as to bind them together. Lay the last two 7″ logs on top of these crossbeams and the top end logs. Build the gable ends up from the short sections of logs which become shorter and shorter as the peak of the gable is approached. Glue or peg the logs which form the gable end together as they

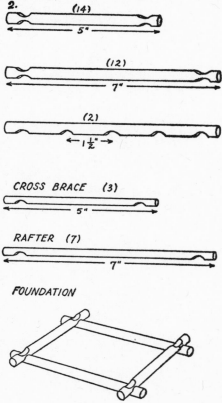

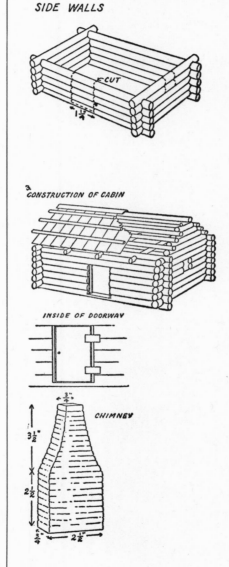

SIDE WALLS

CUT

3.
CONSTRUCTION OF CABIN

INSIDE OF DOORWAY

CHIMNEY

are laid one upon the other. Make one notch at each end of the roof rafters and set them over the logs which form the gable ends. If the topmost roof rafter is not quite high enough to give a gradual slope to the roof, glue a ½" piece of ¼" dowel to the last log of the gable end. Then lay the last rafter over these two pieces.

3. Shape the chimney as shown. Make grooves with a knife or saw to represent logs. If small logs are to be used, build up the chimney in the same way as the cabin was built.

Cover the roof with slabs, which should overlap each other by about ¼". Glue them on and also glue or peg the pieces of ⅛" dowel lengthwise on the roof, three on each side. Soak the ¹⁄₃₂" x ½" x 7" pieces of balsa and bend it around a ⅜" dowel. When dry glue it to the peak of the roof to cover the opening where the slabs meet.

Glue the two sides of the doorframe in place. Drill a no. 60 hole in the door for the latchstring and hang the door on the leather hinges. Cover the window with oiled paper.

A WATER WHEEL AND GRIST MILL

Water, as a source of power, was used by man long before the first settlers landed on the shores of the New World. The colonists in North America used water to drive the great wheels which turned the machinery in the grist mills and in the saw mills. The colonial farmer took his grain to the mill which was built beside a small stream and there it was ground into flour between the heavy, furrowed millstones.

In the middle of the seventeenth century John Winthrop and his neighbors built a grist mill beside Jordan's Brook in New London, Connecticut. This picturesque old mill with its gambrel roof and large water wheel is still standing there—a relic of an age now long since gone.

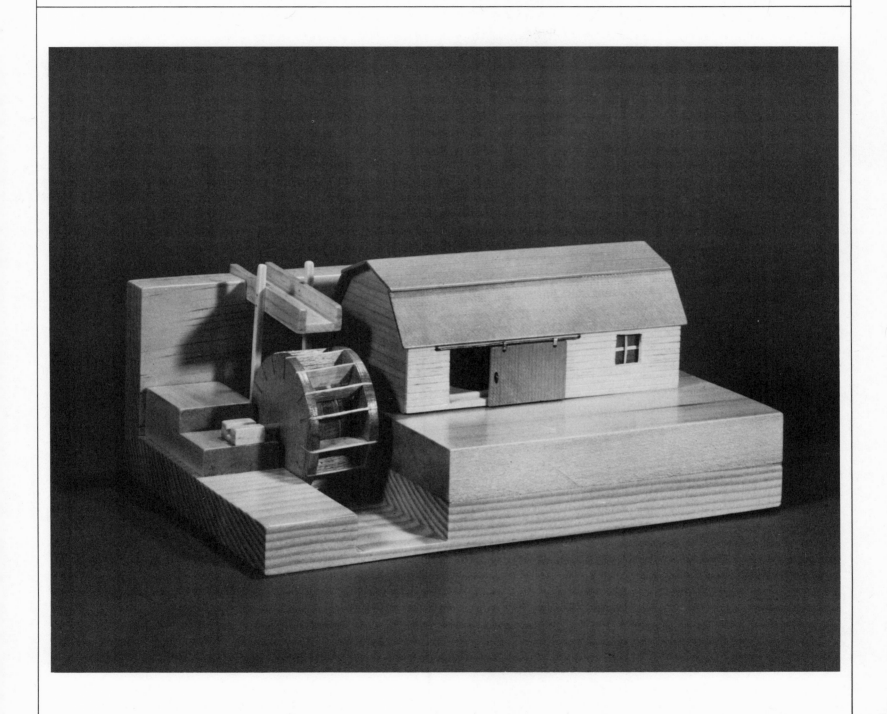

Materials

2 pc ³⁄₁₆″ x 2¼″ x 2½″—ends
2 pc ¹⁄₁₆″ x 1⅛″ x 4½″—sides
1 pc ¹⁄₁₆″ x 2½″ x 4½″—floor
2 pc ¹⁄₁₆″ x ⅞″ x 4¾″—roof—upper slope
2 pc ¹⁄₁₆″ x 1¹⁄₁₆″ x 4¾″—roof—lower slope } mill
1 pc ¹⁄₁₆″ x 1″ x 1⅜″—door
6 pc ¹⁄₃₂″ x ¹⁄₃₂″ x ¾″—window sash
1 pc 20 gauge wire 3″ long—track
2 pc thin metal ¹⁄₁₆″ x ½″—door hangers

2 discs ⅛″ thick and 2¼″ in diameter
16 pc ¹⁄₁₆″ x ⅜″ x 1″—blades } wheel
1 pc ⅛″ dowel 2¾″ long—shaft
1 pc ³⁄₁₆″ x ½″ x ½″—shaft holder

1 pc ⅛″ x ⅝″ x 2½″
2 pc ¹⁄₁₆″ x ⅜″ x 2½″ } mill run
2 pc ³⁄₃₂″ x ³⁄₃₂″ x 3½″—supports

2 pc ¾″ dowel ³⁄₁₆″ long
2 buttonmolds ⅜″ in diameter } grinders

1 pc ¾″ x 6″ x 9″—A
1 pc ¾″ x 6″ x 6″—B
1 pc ¾″ x 1¼″ x 2½″—C } base
1 pc ¾″ x 2½″ x 7″—D

Construction

1. Saw out the ends. Cut out a 1¼″ x ⅞″ opening for the door and ½″ x ½″ openings for windows. The upper edge of each opening should be ¼″ from the top edge of the side section. Make lines or grooves with an awl ⅛″ apart, lengthwise on each side and end to represent the sid-

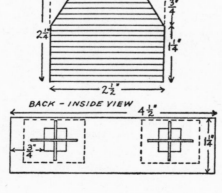

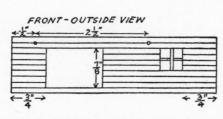

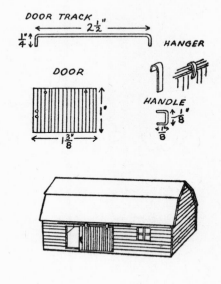

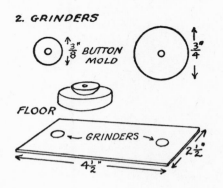

ing boards. Glue two strips, to represent the window sash, to the inside of each side section across each window opening.

Glue the ends to the bottom board and put on the sides. Glue the roof boards on. Fill in the crack at the peak with plastic wood, or glue a ¹⁄₁₆″ x ¹⁄₁₆″ x 4¾″ piece of balsa in the crack and sandpaper it down when dry. Hang the door on a wire track 2½″ long. Make the hangers for the door from copper foil or tin ¹⁄₁₆″ wide and ½″ long. Make no. 60 holes in the door ⅛″ down from the top and ¼″ in from each side for the hangers. Put one end of the hanger in the hole and bend the other end so it fits over the track.

2. Make the grinders by gluing ⅜″ buttonmolds to small checkers or pieces of dowel. Glue them to the floor of the mill.

3. Drill ⅛″ holes through the center of each of the discs to be used for the wheel. Make 16 saw cuts ⅜″ in depth around the circumference of the discs. Saw both discs together so that the cuts correspond with each other. Glue a ¾″ piece cut from a spool

between the discs at the center. Be sure to have the saw cuts opposite each other. Insert the blades into the saw cuts. Put the shaft through the holes in the discs and the hole in the spool. The mill run is made by gluing the sidepieces to the bottom piece.

4. To make the base upon which to mount the mill and the wheel, first make a groove 1½″ in width and ½″ deep 1½″ in from one end of piece A. Make the groove run the full width of the piece. Make saw cuts first and then remove the wood with a chisel. Drill an ⅛″ hole in the center of one end of piece B, ⅛″ down from the top, for the end of the shaft. Then fasten piece B to piece A. Shape piece C as shown and fasten to piece A and B. Then shape piece D and fasten in place. Make a holder in which the end of the shaft can run by filing a groove in a piece ³⁄₁₆″ x ½″ x ½″. Glue the holder to the top of piece D so that the groove will be in line with the hole drilled in piece B for the other end of the shaft. Set the run in the notch cut in C and glue one of the upright supports to each

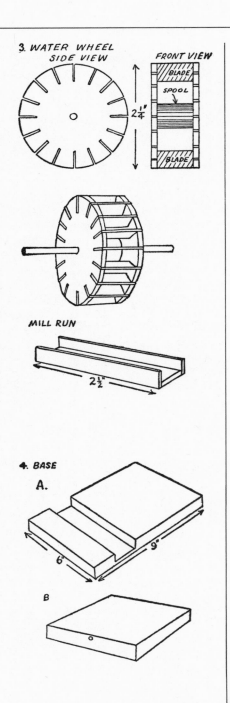

3. WATER WHEEL SIDE VIEW

FRONT VIEW

BLADE

SPOOL

BLADE

2¼″

MILL RUN

2½″

4. BASE

A.

9″

6″

B

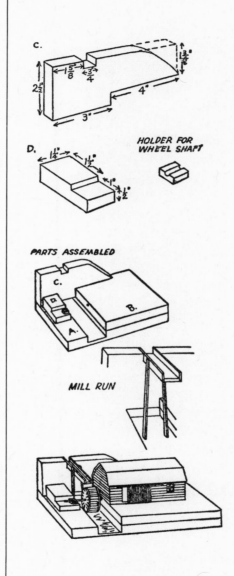

side of the run. Mount the mill on piece B so that the center of the mill is over the end of the shaft.

Stain the model. Use blue paint to represent the water.

A MEETINGHOUSE

The first houses of worship in the New World were made of logs and served as places for meetings other than religious services. They were called meetinghouses, and the people worshiped in them as well. These buildings often had dirt or sanded floors, and the people sat on hard, crude benches. There was no fireplace or chimney, as the meetinghouses were unheated. Many of them were still without a source of heat even into the first part of the nineteenth century.

As time went on, the log buildings were replaced by little clapboarded structures with raftered walls, some pews, benches, and a pulpit.

Materials for main building

2 pc ⅛″ x 3″ x 4″—ends
2 pc 1/16″ x 1¾″ x 5″—sides
1 pc ¼″ x 4″ x 4¾″—floor
2 pc ¼″ x ¼″ x 4¾″—braces
16 pc 1/16″ x ¼″ x 5¼″—roof boards
1 pc ¾″ x ¾″ x 1½″—steeple
1 pc ⅛″ x 1″ x 1½″—door ⎫
1 pc 1/16″ x ⅛″ x 1″—lower support
1 pc ⅛″ x ⅛″ x 1″—upper support
1 pc ⅛″ x 5/16″ x ¾″—sill ⎬ door assembly
2 pc 1/16″ x ⅛″ x 1½″—frame
1 small nail—knob
1 paper clip—hinges ⎭
4 windows

Materials for main building

2 pc $\frac{1}{8}$" x 2" x 2$\frac{1}{2}$"—end, roof support
2 pc $\frac{1}{16}$" x 1$\frac{7}{8}$" x 1$\frac{1}{2}$"—sides
1 pc $\frac{1}{4}$" x 2" x 1$\frac{3}{8}$"—floor
2 pc $\frac{1}{8}$" x $\frac{1}{4}$" x 1$\frac{1}{2}$"—roof support posts
10 pc $\frac{1}{16}$" x $\frac{1}{4}$" x 1$\frac{5}{8}$"—roof boards
1 pc $\frac{1}{8}$" x 1" x 1$\frac{1}{2}$"—door
1 pc $\frac{1}{16}$" x $\frac{1}{8}$" x 1"—lower support
1 pc $\frac{1}{8}$" x $\frac{1}{8}$" x 1"—upper support
1 pc $\frac{1}{16}$" x $\frac{1}{8}$" x $\frac{3}{4}$"—sill
2 pc $\frac{1}{16}$" x $\frac{1}{8}$" x 1$\frac{1}{2}$"—sides } frame
1 pc $\frac{1}{16}$" x $\frac{1}{8}$" x 1$\frac{1}{4}$"—top
1 pc $\frac{1}{4}$" x $\frac{1}{4}$" x 1$\frac{1}{4}$"—step
1 small nail—knob
1 paper clip—hinges
$\frac{1}{32}$" or $\frac{1}{64}$" material—for shingles

door assembly

Construction of main building

1. Make the two end sections as shown in the diagram. Cut a $\frac{3}{4}$" by 1$\frac{3}{4}$" opening for the doorway in one end.

2. Prepare the side sections with two $\frac{3}{8}$" by $\frac{5}{8}$" openings for the windows 1$\frac{1}{8}$" from either end and $\frac{1}{4}$" down from the upper edge.

3. Draw lines with an awl or sharp nail about $\frac{1}{8}$" apart on the ends and sides to represent clapboard siding.

4. Glue the ends to the floor and the braces between them 1$\frac{3}{8}$" up from the floor. See the diagram.

5. Glue the sides to the floor, braces, and ends.

6. Hang the door and install the windows. See the Introduction (pages 6–8).

7. Fasten the doorsill to the end of the floor, and glue the frame pieces to each side of the doorway $\frac{1}{4}$" from the lower edge of the end.

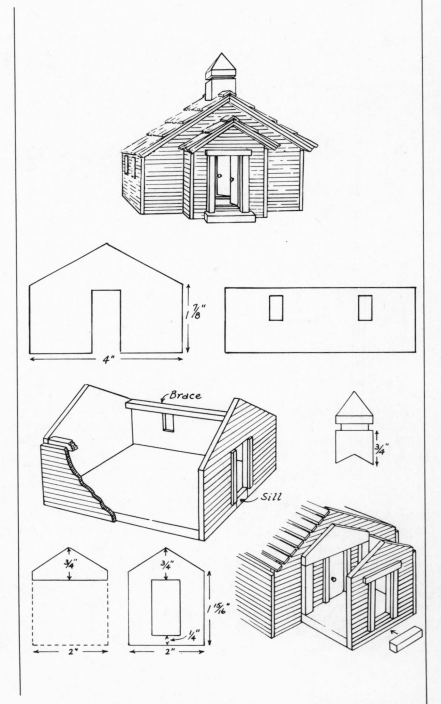

8. Shape the steeple as shown in the diagram. Make the groove around the steeple ¾″ from the end. Make a saw cut to a depth of about ⅛″ and then finish with a file. The notch in the lower end must be the same angle as the roof. Glue the steeple to the roof about ½″ back from the front end after the roof boards have been put on.

Construction of Vestibule

1. Make two end sections as shown. Cut a ¾″ by 1½″ opening for the doorway in one end.

2. Draw lines to represent clapboards on the doorway end and the sides. Glue the end piece to the end of the floor.

3. Hang the door and set the sill in place against the lower door support.

4. Cut a ¾″ piece from the peak end of the remaining end piece to make the vestibule roof support. See the diagram.

5. Center the roof support on the doorway end of the building with the lower edge along the upper edge of the doorway and resting on the door frame. The peak should be down ½″ from the peak of the main building and in line with it.

6. Glue the supporting posts to the end of the building as shown.

7. Glue the sides to the end, posts, and floor.

8. Frame the door. Glue the step to the end of the vestibule in front of the doorway.

9. Put the roof boards on both parts of the building. Box in the ends of the boards and shingle the roof. See the Introduction (pages 8–10).

AN OLD DISTRICT SCHOOLHOUSE

The one-room schoolhouse, once so common in our country, is fast disappearing from the American scene. District schoolhouses were built during the eighteenth and nineteenth centuries, and many were in use until well into the twentieth century.

These old-time schoolhouses were, as a rule, built near the geographical center of the district on a site that had little value for anything else. They were heated by a large fireplace or stove, with wood often provided by the parents of the pupils.

The furnishings in the schoolroom were meager, usually made by a local carpenter. In some schools the children sat on backless benches, while others had a shelf on three sides of the room with benches for the older pupils. In other schoolrooms crude desks were built for the children.

Materials

2 pc 1/8″ x 2 1/2″ x 3″—ends
2 pc 1/16″ x 1 9/16″ x 5″—sides
1 pc 1/4″ x 3″ x 4 3/4″—floor
1 pc 1/8″ x 2 1/4″ x 3″—partition
12 pc 1/16″ x 1/4″ x 5 1/4″—roof boards
1/64″ or 1/32″ material—for shingles

Door assemblies:
2 pc 1/8″ x 5/8″ x 1″—doors
2 pc 1/16″ x 1/8″ x 5/8″—bottom supports
2 pc 1/8″ x 1/8″ x 5/8″—top supports
2 pc 1/16″ x 1/8″ x 1″—sides } frame, outer door
1 pc 1/16″ x 1/8″ x 7/8″—top } frame, outer door
1 pc 1/16″ x 1/8″ x 1/2″—sill, outer door
1 pc 1/16″ x 3/16″ x 1/2″—threshold, inner door
2 small nails—knobs
2 pins

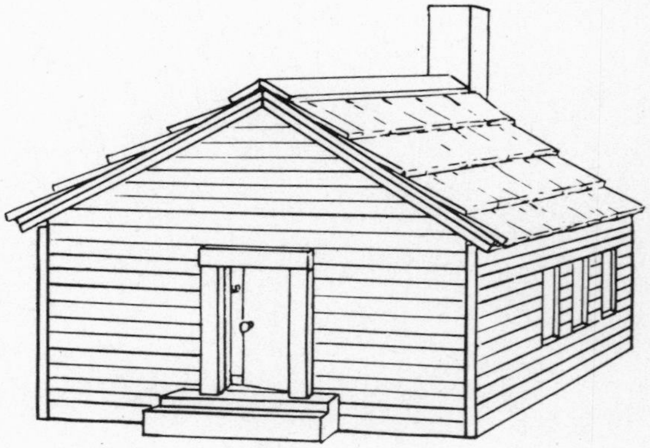

1 pc ⅜″ x ½″ x 3½″—chimney
1 pc ¼″ x ⅜″ x 1¼″—A ⎫
1 pc ⅛″ x ¼″ x 1¼″—B ⎭ steps
12 flat toothpicks—pegs

Construction

1. Using the drawing as a guide, make the end sections. Cut a ½″ by 1″ opening in the center of one end for the doorway.

2. Cut out the partition, which is ¼″ narrower than the end sections. Make the ½″ by 1″ doorway ½″ from one end of the partition. Drill twelve holes ¼″ apart for pegs to hang hats and coats on. See the diagram.

3. Prepare the side sections. See the diagram for the location of the window openings, which are ⅝″ in height and ⅜″ in width.

4. Draw lines with an awl or nail about ⅛″ apart on the outside of the ends and sides to represent clapboard siding.

5. Glue the end sections to the ends of the floorboard.

6. Glue the sides to the ends and floor.

7. Insert short toothpick pegs into the holes in the partition. Glue the partition between the sides and to the floor 1″ from the inside of the doorway end of the building.

8. Drill a hole for the knob in each door ⅛″ from the edge, opposite the holes for the "hinges" and ⅜″ from the lower end. Hang the doors and install the windows. See the Introduction (pages 6–8).).

9. Glue the doorsill against the lower door support, and glue the threshold to the floor and lower support for inside door.

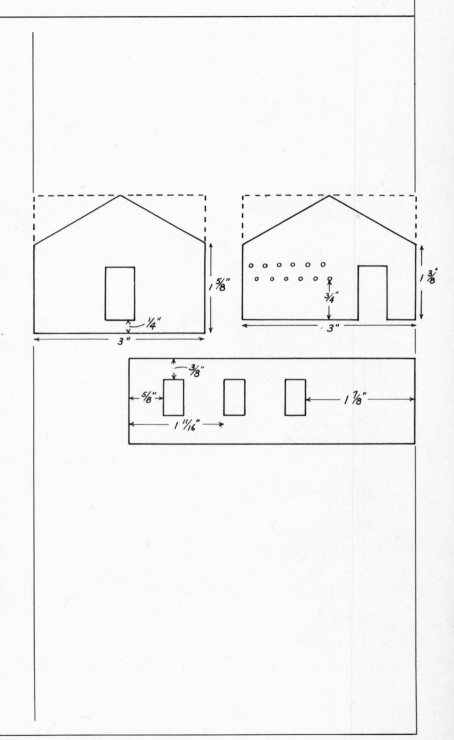

10. Glue the doorframe to the sides and along the upper edge of the doorway.

11. Glue the chimney to the center of the back end of the schoolhouse.

12. Put the roof boards on, box in the ends, and shingle the roof. See the Introduction (pages 8–10).

13. Construct the steps by gluing the B piece to the A piece. Center the steps in front of the doorway and glue them to the end of the building.

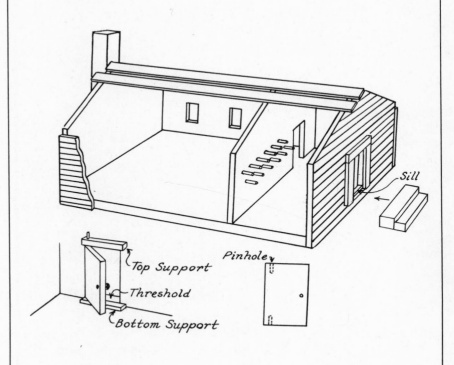

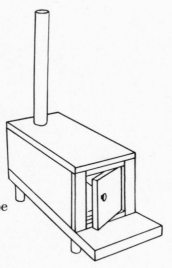

A WOODBURNING STOVE

Materials

1 pc ¼″ x 1⅝″ x 3¾″—base
4 pc ³⁄₁₆″ dowel ¾″ long—legs
2 pc ⅛″ x 1½″ x 3″—sides
1 pc ¼″ x 1½″ x 1¼″—end
2 pc ¼″ x ¼″ x 1¼″—cross braces
1 pc ⅛″ x 1½″ x 3⅛″—top
1 pc ¼″ dowel 2½″ long—stovepipe
2 pc ⅛″ x ¼″ x 1½″—A
2 pc ⅛″ x ⅛″ x 1″—door supports
1 pc ⅛″ x 1″ x 1¼″—door
1 pin or round toothpick—door handle
1 paper clip

Construction

1. Glue the sides to the end.

2. Glue the two cross braces between the sides at the opposite end. See the diagram.

3. Drill four ³⁄₁₆″ holes in the base for the legs. The holes are ¼″ from the side edges, ½″ from one end and 1″ from the other end.

4. Insert the legs into the holes.

5. Glue an A piece to the end of each side and the cross braces.

6. Glue door supports to the two cross braces. The upper support will be even with the upper edge of the brace while the lower support will be even with the lower edge of that brace.

7. Set the door temporarily in place and drill a small hole ¼″ in depth through each support and into the door about ¹⁄₁₆″ from the ends of the supports and door.

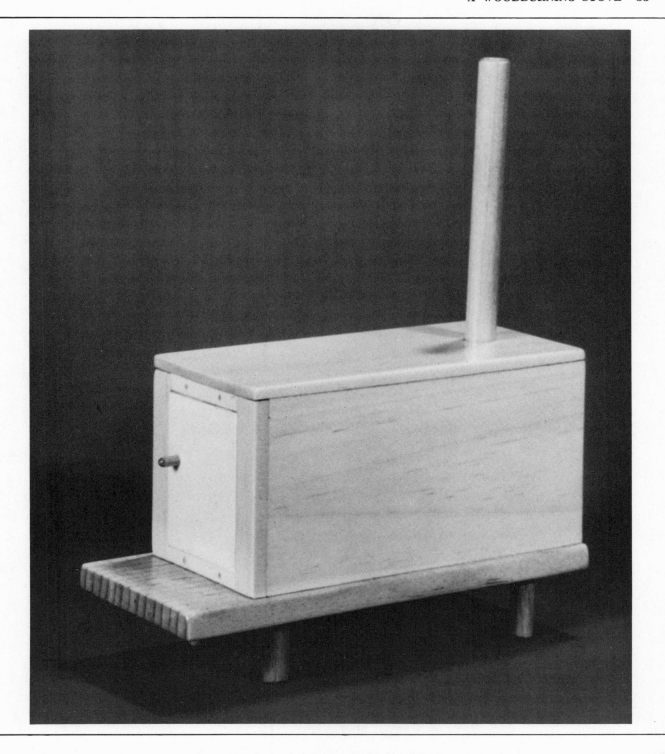

8. Round off the inside edge of the door on the side where the holes were drilled.

9. Drill a hole in the door for the handle, which can be a piece of round toothpick or a piece cut from a pin.

10. Insert pieces of wire about ⅜″ in length through the door supports and into the holes in the door.

11. Glue the body of the stove to the base, which will extend ⅝″ at the door or front end.

12. Make a ¼″ hole ½″ from one end of the top and midway between the side edges for the stovepipe.

13. Fasten the top on the stove.

14. Paint the stove and pipe black.

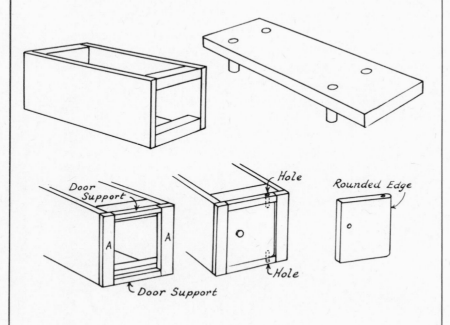

BARNS—THEN AND NOW

Various types of barns were built in America, depending on the use to which they were put and the building materials available in the area. In Pennsylvania, stone was used extensively in the construction of barns, and many old barns made partly or entirely of stone are still to be found there.

The framework for the barns was prepared and partially assembled on the ground. When all was ready, the neighbors for miles around gathered for the barn "raising." The parts of the frame were fitted together and held in place with wooden pins or trunnels.

Every effort has been made to simplify the construction of the barn, yet have the finished model as realistic as possible. Due to varying thicknesses or slight differences in length or width of materials used, minor adjustments will have to be made from time to time as the model is being constructed.

Builders of earlier days fastened their barns together with mortise and tenon joints and trunnels or treenails. In building the models, glue takes the place of the mortise and tenon and toothpicks are the trunnels.

AN OLD STONE BARN

Materials

2 pc ¼″ x ¼″ x 6″—A } sills
2 pc ¼″ x ¼″ x 2½″—B

4 pc ⅛″ x ¼″ x 1½″ } post spacers
2 pc ⅛″ x ¼″ x 2″

8 pc ¼″ x ¼″ x 2½″—braces } frame sections
8 pc ¼″ x ¼″ x 2¾″—posts

7 pc ⅛″ x ¼″ x 2½″—floor joists

5 pc ⅛″ x ½″ x 5½″—flooring

2 pc ¼″ x 3″ x 6″—side forms

2 pc ¼″ x 3½″ x 5″—end forms

2 pc ¼″ x ¼″ x 2½″—top, bottom } doorframe
2 pc ¼″ x ¼″ x 2⅛″—sides

1 pc ¼″ x ⅜″ x 2″—filler

2 pc ¼″ x 1″ x 2⅛″—doors }
4 pc ⅛″ x ⅛″ x ⅞″—hinges } door assembly
2 pc ¹⁄₁₆″ x ⅛″ x ½″—handles
2 paper clips

5 pc ⅛″ x ¼″ x 3″—A }
2 pc ⅛″ x ¼″ x 2⅞″—B } rafters
3 pc ⅛″ x ¼″ x 2¾″—C
6 pc ¹⁄₁₆″ x ¼″ x 2½″—braces

2 pc ⅛″ x ¼″ x 6″—plates

1 pc ¼″ x ¼″ x 2″—X, brace above doorway

8 pc ⅛″ x ¼″ x 1¹³⁄₃₂″—rafter spacers

20 pc ¹⁄₁₆″ x ¼″ x 7¼″—roof boards

4 pc ¹⁄₁₆″ x ½″ x length required } to box in ends
4 pc ¹⁄₁₆″ x ⅛″ x length required

¹⁄₃₂″ material (or ¹⁄₆₄″ if available)—for shingles

Construction

1. Make the sills by gluing the B pieces between the A pieces. Check with the try square to make sure that the corners are square.

2. Set the floor joists in place ¾″ apart. Also glue a joist to the inside of each end sill for the flooring to rest on.

3. Draw a line across each of eight of the posts 1¼″ from one end (lower). Glue a cross brace between each of the four pairs of posts 1¼″ up, using the lines as guides to locate the brace. Fasten another brace between the posts at the upper end.

4. Glue one end frame section to the sills, then 1½″ spacers, another frame section, the 2″ spacers, then the remaining pair of 1½″ spacers and the last frame section. Make sure that the frame sections are in a straight line and perpendicular to the sills.

5. Lay the flooring.

6. Cut an opening 2″ wide and 2¼″ high in one of the side forms for the doorway.

7. Make the end forms.

8. Glue the side forms to the posts and sills. Fasten the end forms in place. On the inside of the form with the doorway, glue brace X between the two middle frame sections and even with the upper edge of the doorway.

9. Prepare a mixture of shredded papier-mâché and cover the inside of the barn except the floor, to a depth of $\frac{3}{16}$″ to ¼″. Fill in between the posts and braces, leaving them exposed. Press small pieces of stone into the mixture.

10. Cover the outside of the forms the same way. Before pressing pieces of stone into the ends, mark the location of the vent slits. When the material is partly set, make the slits with a blunt end tool such as a screwdriver. Use a thinner coating, or about ⅛″ in depth, along the upper

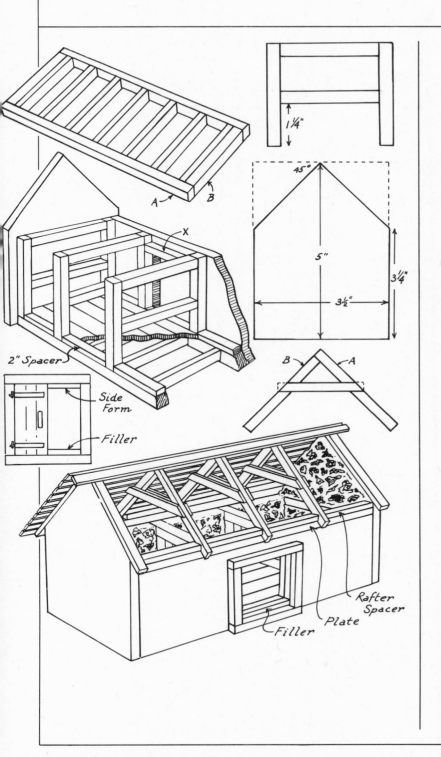

2" Spacer

Side Form

Filler

45°

5"

3¼"

3½"

1¼"

A

B

X

B

A

Rafter Spacer

Plate

Filler

side edges so as not to interfere with the rafters when they are put in.

11. Make three rafter assemblies by gluing the B pieces to the A pieces and putting a brace on each side. Cut off the protruding ends of the braces. Glue the other four rafters to the gable ends of the forms, allowing the A piece to overlap the B piece at the peak. These rafters should be glued to the forms with the wider side on the forms.

12. Fasten the plates to the edges of the side forms. Glue the spacers to the plates, starting at one end, and leaving a ⅛″ opening between each spacer for the rafters to fit into. Install the rafters, making sure that they are in line with the two end peaks.

13. Put on the roof boards and shingle the roof; then hang the doors. See the Introduction (pages 7–10).

Note: The construction of this barn may be simplified by leaving out the rafters and just gluing the roof boards to the end sections.

A SALT BOX HOUSE
(DOLL HOUSE)

The lean-to house, often called the "salt box" house, was a familiar sight in New England. Many of these old houses are still in existence today and are examples of one type of architecture in early New England. These old houses sometimes began as a single room dwelling and were added to as the family increased in numbers and more room was required.

The model of the old salt-box house can be enlarged to make a doll house by multiplying each dimension, except the thickness, by 8 and adding partitions. This will make a house 33″ high by 38″ wide by 40″ long or to a scale of 1″ to 1′. If a smaller house is desired multiply by 4 instead of 8. For a doll house use ½″ or ¾″ stock for the ends, partitions and lower floor. The partitions should be the thickness of the floor narrower than the end pieces. Use ¼″ stock for the upper floors, front, back and roof. Omit the cross braces.

The upper floors can be supported by gluing strips on the inside of the end pieces and each side of the partitions or grooves can be cut for the floor pieces to fit into.

The front of the house can be made in two sections and hinged at each end. If this is done, the front roof piece cannot extend down over the front as in the model, and the front of the house can be a little higher. Or, the rear roof can be made in two pieces, the upper piece being about 2″ wide. The lower roof section can be hinged to the upper or omitted entirely leaving the back open for ready access to the rooms.

The windows can be drawn or painted on the house or openings can be cut and covered with plastic. See introduction pgs. 7–10. A doorway can be cut out and a hinged door installed, or a door can be glued to the front and framed.

Or, the model itself can be the one-room house of a very small doll. In this case the rear roof piece at the peak should be about 1½″ wide and the rest of the roof left off or hinged to the upper piece.

Materials

2 pc ⅛″ x 4⅛″ x 4¾″—ends
1 pc ¼″ x 4¾″ x 4¾″—floor
1 pc ⅛″ x 2¼″ x 5″—front
1 pc ⅛″ x 1¹¹⁄₁₆″ x 5″—back
1 pc ⅛″ x 3″ x 5¼″—front ⎱ roof
1 pc ⅛″ x 4½″ x 5¼″—back ⎰
2 pc ¹⁄₃₂″ x ³⁄₁₆″ x 2¼″—back ⎱ ridge boards
2 pc ¹⁄₃₂″ x ¼″ x 2¼″—front ⎰
6 pc ¼″ x ¼″ x 4¾″—cross braces
1 pc ⅛″ x ⅝″ x ⅞″—door
1 pc ¹⁄₁₆″ x ⅛″ x ¾″—lower ⎱ door supports
1 pc ⅛″ x ⅛″ x ¾″—upper ⎰
3 pc ¹⁄₃₂″ x ⅛″ x ¹¹⁄₁₆″—door frame
1 pc ⅛″ x ⅛″ x ¾″ ⎱ steps
1 pc ⅛″ x ⁵⁄₁₆″ x ¾″ ⎰
1 pc ½″ x ¾″ x ¾″—chimney

Construction

1. Saw out the end pieces as shown in the diagram so that the grain of the wood will simulate horizontal siding. Select wood with a fine grain, if possible, or lines may be made with a sharp awl to represent siding.

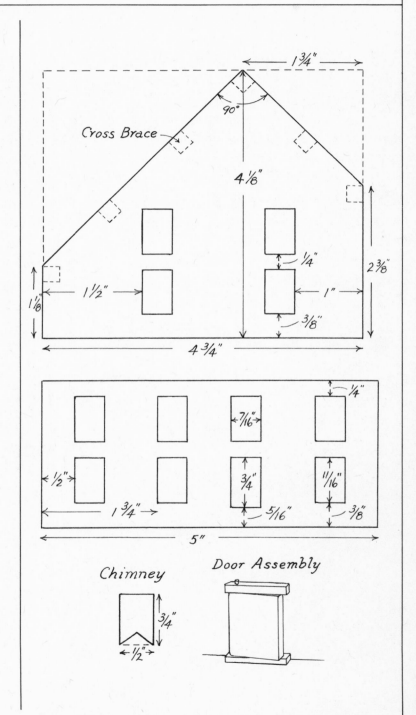

Cross Brace

Chimney

Door Assembly

2. With a sharp knife cut out the openings for the windows and doorway. The window openings will depend on the size of windows used. Cut the openings a little smaller than needed and finish to desired size with a flat file so as to get a tight fit.

3. Install the windows in the ends and front section. Make and install the door assembly. The lower door support should be glued to the inside of the front ¼″ up from the lower edge. See introduction pgs. 7–10.

4. Glue the end sections to the floor and the braces between the ends. See diagram.

5. Glue the front and back sections to the floor, braces and ends. Also glue the lower door support to the floor.

6. Make and glue the steps in place. Frame the doorway.

7. Glue the front roof piece to the ends and braces letting it extend ⅛″ beyond the peak.

8. Glue the rear roof section to the ends, braces and against the front piece at the peak.

9. Glue the chimney to the center of the roof.

10. Shingle the house. See introduction pgs. 7–10.

FURNISHINGS IN MINIATURE

A SETTLE

Alongside the great fireplaces in the kitchens of colonial America usually stood the settle, a simply constructed piece of furniture, but very well adapted for use in those days. It had a high back and a seat, the front of which went all the way down to the floor. The settle, thus constructed, kept the cold drafts out and the heat from the fireplace in. Some settles were made with a chest beneath the seat for the storage of whatever articles the housewife wished to keep there.

Materials

2 pc $\frac{1}{16}$″ x 1″ x 3½″—ends
1 pc $\frac{1}{16}$″ x 1″ x 2½″—front
2 pc $\frac{1}{16}$″ x 1″ x 2⅜″—seat and bottom
4 pc $\frac{1}{16}$″ x ⅛″ x ⅞″—seat and bottom supports
1 pc $\frac{1}{16}$″ x ½″ x 2½″—top
1 pc $\frac{1}{16}$″ x 2½″ x 3½″—back

Construction

1. Saw out the end sections as shown in the diagram. Glue the seat and bottom supports to the inside of the end sections. The bottom support is ⅛″ from the lower end and the support for the seat is ⅞″ from the same end. Glue the bottom board in place between the ends. Put on the front piece.

2. Cut the seat board lengthwise into two pieces—one ¾" wide and one piece ¼" wide. Glue the ¼" piece in place. The front part of the seat is just set in place and can be removed, as the lower part of the settle was often used as a chest for storage.

3. Notch out the top piece as shown and glue in place.

4. Cut the back section lengthwise into four parts each ⅝" x 3½". Apply glue to the back edges of the top, the end sections and the bottom. Fit the back boards in place.

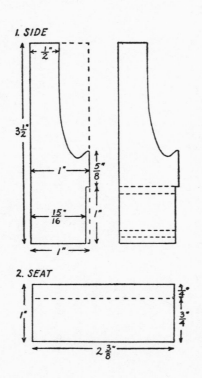

I. SIDE

2. SEAT

3. TOP

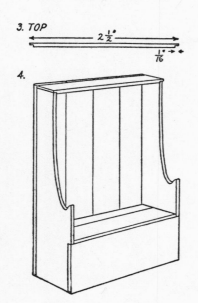

4.

A BUTTER CHURN

In the corner of many a colonial kitchen stood a wooden churn with a long handle, on the lower end of which was a wooden dasher. The making of butter was one of the duties of the women and girls of the eighteenth century and many an hour was spent moving the dasher up and down in the cream until butter was formed. Then cold water was poured into the churn, the dasher was turned and the butter was thus "gathered" and removed from the churn, leaving buttermilk behind. The butter was then worked in the wooden butter bowl and pressed into butter molds, after which it was ready for eating.

Materials

1 pc dowel or round stick 1¼″ in diameter and 2¼″ long—barrel or churn (A piece of broom handle or window shade roller may be used, or the barrel may be shaped from a piece of balsa. The dimensions given make a good model although it can be larger or smaller.)

1 pc applicator 4¼″ long ⎫ dasher
2 pc ⅟₁₆″ x ³⁄₃₂″ x ¾″ ⎭ dasher

3 pc ⅟₃₂″ x ¼″ x 4″—bands around churn

1 disc ⅟₁₆″ thick and 1″ in diameter—cover

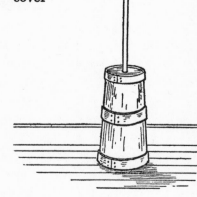

Construction

1. Drill a ¾″ hole down through the center of the round stick or dowel to within ¼″ of the bottom or 2″ deep. With a knife, file, and sandpaper, shape the barrel as shown in the diagram. It should be about 1″ in diameter at the top and 1¼″ at the bottom. Soak the bands of balsa and put them around the churn one at the top, one at the bottom, and one in the middle. Allow the top band to extend ⅛″ above the top of the barrel and so form a place for the cover. Hold the bands in place with rubber bands until dry, then cement the ends together. Again use the rubber bands until the cement sets.

2. Drill a no. 43 hole in the center of the cover. Drill no. 45 holes in the center of the dasher paddles. Glue these pieces to the handle so as to make a cross. Put the dasher into the barrel and put on the cover.

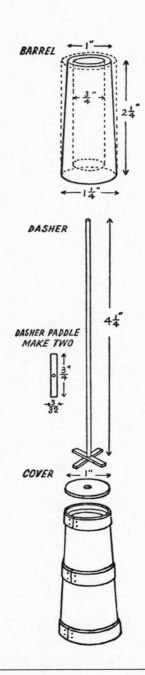

BARREL

DASHER

DASHER PADDLE
MAKE TWO

COVER

A WOOL WHEEL

The whirr of the wool wheel was a familiar sound in the homes of early America. The women and girls spun all the yarn which was later made into clothing for the entire family. The wool wheel, also called the great wheel, replaced the distaff and hand spindle and was a far more efficient means of spinning. The spinner stood beside the large wheel and made it rotate by striking the spokes with a wooden stick. A cord or belt connected the large wheel with a pulley on the spindle, which was mounted on a post at the other end of the spinning wheel. When the wheel was rotated by the spinner the spindle, on which the yarn was wound, revolved very rapidly. Spinning wheels were in use in most homes in America until about a hundred years ago and can still be found in many an attic.

Materials

1 pc $\frac{3}{16}''$ x $\frac{3}{4}''$ x 6"—base
2 pc $\frac{1}{8}''$ dowel $1\frac{1}{2}''$ long—back leg
1 pc $\frac{1}{8}''$ dowel 2" long—front leg
1 embroidery hoop about 5" in diameter—large wheel
1 pc $\frac{3}{8}''$ dowel $\frac{3}{4}''$ long—hub
1 pc applicator $1\frac{1}{4}''$ long—axle
12 pc applicator $2\frac{1}{4}''$ long—spokes
1 pc $\frac{1}{4}''$ dowel 4" long—wheel post
1 pc $\frac{1}{4}''$ dowel 3" long—spindle post
1 pc $\frac{1}{4}''$ dowel $1\frac{1}{2}''$ long—spindle holder
1 pc $\frac{1}{8}''$ dowel $\frac{1}{4}''$ long—pulley
2 pc $\frac{1}{8}''$ dowel $1\frac{1}{4}''$ long—upright posts
1 pin or wire 2" long—spindle (Hat pin or corsage pin may be used.)
2 pc leather about $\frac{1}{32}''$ x $\frac{1}{16}''$ x 1"

Construction

1. Shape the wheel post and the spindle post as shown. Taper the lower ends to about ⅛″ in diameter. Drill a no. 45 hole ½″ down from the top of the wheel post. Make the groove in the wheel post with a file. The groove is ¼″ down from the top. Make spindle post and 3 legs as shown in diagrams.

2. Drill ³⁄₁₆″ holes in the base at X and Y for the posts, and no. 43 holes at A, B, C, for the legs. Drill the holes so that the legs and posts will set into the base at an angle. The hole for the wheel post at Y is off center and should be ½″ in from the front edge of the base, and 1¾″ from the end. The hole for the spindle post at X is in the center of the base and 1¼″ in from the other end. Set the posts and legs in the holes.

3. Make the wheel. Shape the hub as shown. Make the groove with a small round file before sawing the ¾″ piece off. Drill a no. 43 hole through the center of the hub. Drill a no. 60 hole ⅛″ in from one end of the axle. Insert the other end of the axle into the hole in the wheel post. Put

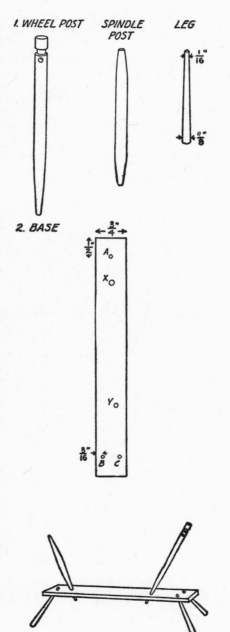

1. WHEEL POST   SPINDLE POST   LEG

2. BASE

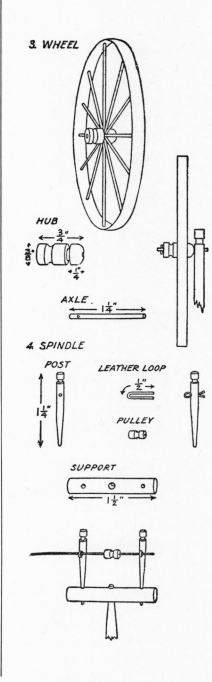

3. WHEEL

HUB

$\frac{3}{4}''$

$\frac{3}{4}''$

$\frac{1}{4}''$

AXLE. $1\frac{1}{4}''$

4. SPINDLE

POST

$1\frac{1}{4}''$

LEATHER LOOP

$\frac{1}{2}''$

PULLEY

SUPPORT

$1\frac{1}{2}''$

the wheel on the axle and put a peg in the hole in the axle to hold it on.

4. Drill no. 43 holes ¼″ in from each end of the spindle support for the two upright posts which are shaped from 1¼″ pieces of ⅛″ dowel. Also drill an ⅛″ hole in the spindle support equidistant from each end. Drill no. 45 holes ⅜″ down from the top of these two posts for the leather loops in which the spindle will turn. Insert the posts into the holes made in the spindle support.

Make the pulley from a ¼″ piece of ⅛″ dowel through which a pinhole has been drilled lengthwise. Put the pulley on the spindle and fasten the spindle to the posts with loops made from very thin leather or black paper or cloth. Set the spindle assembly on the spindle post. Run a thread or string around the pulley and the large wheel.

A FOOT STOVE

In colonial days in America women and children carried foot stoves to church with them, because the unheated churches were cold and damp, and the sermons were long. These little stoves were wooden boxes or wooden frames, with a metal box or can inside to hold hot coals. Holes, usually in the form of circles or hearts, were made in the sides, ends and top of the box to allow the heat from the coals to escape.

Materials
1 pc ⅛" x 2⅛" x 3"—front
1 pc ⅛" x 2" x 3"—back
2 pc ⅛" x 2" x 2¼"—ends
2 pc ⅛" x 3" x 3½"—top and bottom
1 pc 20 gauge wire 5" long

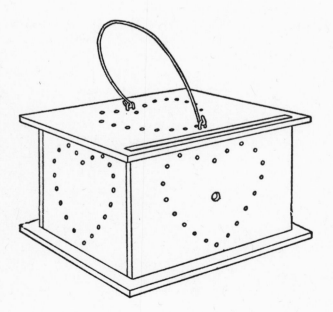

Construction

1. Saw out the parts as listed. Make a pattern of a heart and use it to draw the outline of a heart on the front piece. Place the pattern equidistant from the edges. Mark the holes as shown and drill holes about $\frac{1}{16}$" in diameter. These holes were to allow the heat to escape. Also drill an $\frac{1}{8}$" hole in the center of this piece.

Use the heart outlined on front piece as pattern to make hearts on the back, top and ends. Do not make the hole in the center of these pieces, however. Lay the front section on the other pieces so that the heart will be equidistant from the sides in each case. Mark through the holes with an awl to make the outline of the heart. Drill $\frac{1}{16}$" holes.

2. Make an opening 3" long and $\frac{1}{8}$" wide in the top section $\frac{1}{4}$" in from the front edge and $\frac{1}{4}$" in from each end. The front piece will slide up and down through this opening.

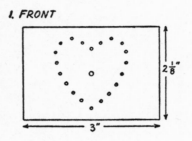

1. FRONT

$2\frac{1}{8}$"

3"

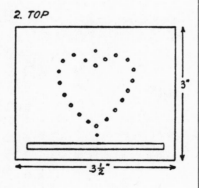

2. TOP

3"

$3\frac{1}{2}$"

3. HANDLE

← 2″ →

3. Drill two small holes for the hooks or screw eyes which will hold the wire handle. Make the handle and fasten it to the top with tiny screw eyes or wire hooks. Shape the handle by bending it around a can about 2″ in diameter.

4. FRONT VIEW

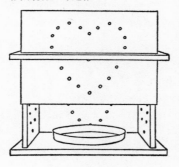

4. Glue the back to the ends. Glue the bottom and the top to the ends and back. The top and bottom will extend ¼″ all around. When putting the top on, insert the front into the opening in the top so that it will slide up and down and will thus determine the exact position of the top. Set a metal can or bottle top about 1½″ in diameter inside the stove to hold the coals.

A CRADLE

The babies of colonial America were usually rocked to sleep in a homemade cradle. The cradle is a very ancient piece of furniture and has been in use throughout the world for many centuries. Our colonial forefathers made various types of cradles, some with canopies and some without, some large enough for twins, one in each end, and some big enough for only one small occupant. On the whole, the cradles were simple but sturdily built articles of furniture and many a pioneer baby slept or played in his homemade bed near the great kitchen fireplace while his mother spun thread for his clothing on her spinning wheel.

Materials

2 pc $\frac{1}{16}''$ x $1\frac{1}{2}''$ x $2''$—ends
2 pc $\frac{1}{16}''$ x $1''$ x $3\frac{1}{2}''$—sides
1 pc $\frac{1}{16}''$ x $1\frac{1}{4}''$ x $3\frac{1}{2}''$—bottom
2 pc $\frac{1}{16}''$ x $\frac{5}{8}''$ x $3''$—rockers
1 pc $\frac{1}{8}''$ x $\frac{1}{8}''$ x $3''$—brace

Construction

1. Cut out the sides and bottom. Trace the drawing for one half of the end on a piece of tracing paper. Fold the paper on the dotted line and cut out.

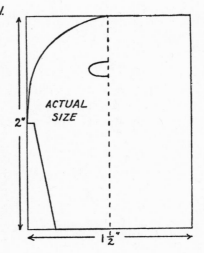

ACTUAL SIZE

2"

$1\frac{1}{2}''$

2. To make the ends draw a light line across the center of the piece from which the end is to be sawed. Measure in ¹⁄₁₆″ from each end of this line and make a dot. Connect this dot with another dot made ¼″ in from each edge at the bottom of the piece.

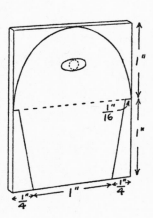

Lay the paper pattern on the board so that the straight edges of the pattern coincide with the lines drawn on the wood. Saw out, then round off the curved edge with fine sandpaper. Drill a no. 43 hole in each end and ½″ from the top. Enlarge hole to correct shape with small round file. Glue the side boards to the end-pieces. Glue on the bottom.

3. Make the rockers by tracing the drawing for one half of a rocker on tracing paper. Fold the paper on the dotted line and cut out the pattern. Lay the pattern on the piece of wood so that the straight edge of the pattern coincides with one edge of the board. Draw around the pattern. Saw out, then round off the curved surface of the rocker with sandpaper.

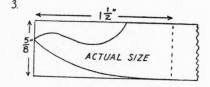

ACTUAL SIZE

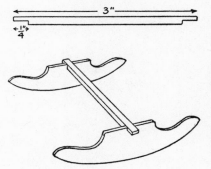

Make a file cut ⅛″ wide and ⅟₁₆″ deep in the center of the top edge of each rocker. Shape the brace as shown in the diagram. Set the brace into the openings made in the rockers. Glue or peg this assembly to the bottom of the cradle equidistant from the sides and ends. Stain the model.

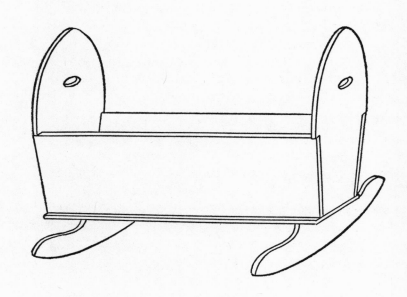

TWO OLD TABLES

A trestle table was one of the most common pieces of furniture in the early seventeenth century home. These tables, measuring some four to six feet in length, were usually made of pine or with a pine top and an understructure of hard wood. The top was made from two wide boards with cleats at each end and with two trestles to support it. The trestles were connected by a flat stretcher between the uprights. Most of the tables, often heavy and crude, were homemade in country and frontier areas.

Another piece of furniture was the hutch table, which served as a table, chair, or settle. There was also space beneath the seat, which was used as a storage compartment. The table top was held in place by wooden pegs and could be tipped down to form a table or raised to serve as the back of a chair or settle.

A TRESTLE TABLE AND BENCHES

Materials for table

2 pc ¼″ x ⅞″ x 4½″—top
2 pc ⅛″ x ¼″ x 1¾″—cleats
2 pc ¼″ x ⅞″ x 1″—upright ⎫
2 pc ¼″ x ⅜″ x 1½″—top supports ⎬ trestles
2 pc ¼″ x ⅜″ x 1⅝″—bottom pc or feet ⎭
1 pc ⅛″ x ¼″ x 4″—stretcher
2 round toothpicks

Construction

1. Glue the two planks for the table top together and add the cleats at the ends of the planks.

2. Make a notch ⅛″ wide and ¼″ deep in the center of each upright piece.

3. Center and glue the upright piece on the top and bottom pieces of the trestle, rounding off the corners as shown.

4. Glue the completed trestles to the underside of the top ½″ in from the ends.

5. Insert the stretcher through the notches allowing it to extend about ¼″ at each end. Mark the position of holes for pegs, remove stretcher, and drill holes for toothpick pegs. Replace the stretcher and insert short pieces of toothpicks into each hole.

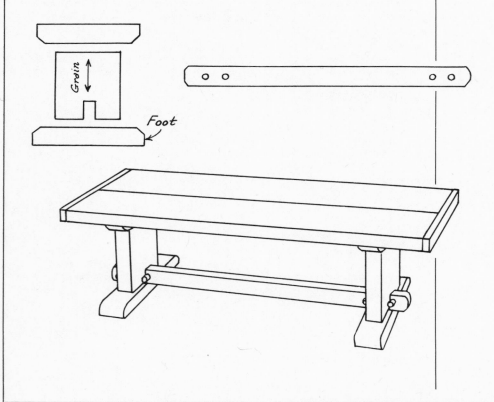

Materials for benches

    2 pc ¼″ x ¾″ x 4″—seat
    4 pc ¼″ x ½″ x ¾″—legs
    4 pc ⅟₁₆″ x ¼″ x 3″—braces

Construction

    1. Glue the legs to the underside of the seat ⅝″ in from either end.
    2. Glue the braces to the legs.

A HUTCH TABLE, SETTLE, AND CHEST

Materials

    2 pc ³⁄₁₆″ x 1″ x 1½″—ends of settle
    1 pc ³⁄₁₆″ x ¾″ x 2¼″—bottom ⎫
    2 pc ⅛″ x ¾″ x ⁹⁄₁₆″—ends   ⎬ chest
    2 pc ⅟₁₆″ x ¾″ x 2¼″—sides ⎭
    1 pc ⅛″ x 1″ x 2¼″   ⎫
    2 pc ⅟₁₆″ x ³⁄₁₆″ x ¾″—A ⎬ seat
    2 pc ⅛″ x 1¼″ x 3⅜″   ⎫
    2 pc ⅛″ x ⅛″ x 2½″—end cleats ⎬ table top
    2 pc ³⁄₁₆″ x ⅜″ x 2″—cross braces
    1 round toothpick

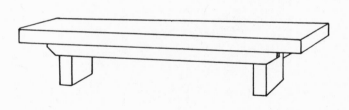

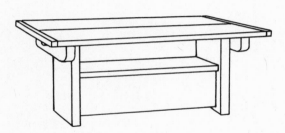

Construction

1. Prepare the ends for the settle as shown. Drill a hole for a toothpick dowel ¼″ down from the upper edge and ⅛″ in from the back edge. It is a good idea to drill the two pieces together before shaping them.

2. Make the chest by gluing the ends to the bottom and then adding the sides.

3. Glue the chest between the ends ⅛″ up from the lower edge and even with the back edges of the ends.

4. Fasten the A pieces to the underside of the seat ⅛″ in from the ends and sides.

5. Drill a hole for a toothpick dowel in each cross brace ⅝″ from one end and ¼″ from one side edge. Round off the corners as shown in the diagram.

6. Glue the table top sections together and fasten the cleats to the ends.

7. Draw light lines on the underside of the table top ½″ in from either end. Using these lines as guides, glue the cross braces to the table top ¼″ in from the side edges. Be sure that the cross braces are 2⅝″ (length of settle) apart as the settle will fit in between the braces. (The braces will be ⁵⁄₁₆″ in from either end.)

8. Put the dowels through the braces and holes in ends of settle. The top should swing back easily on the dowels. If it does not, round off the back corners of the ends of the settle a little more.

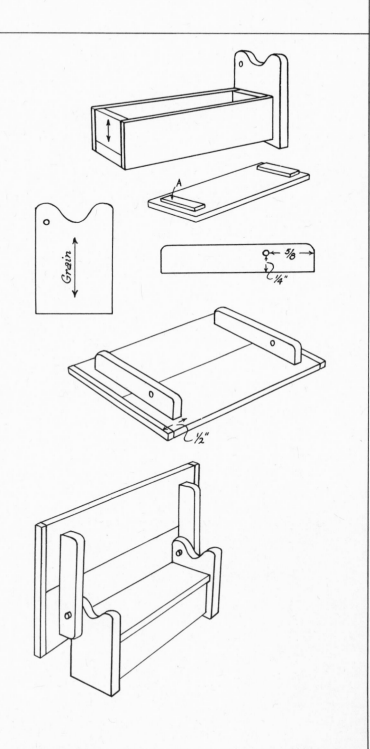

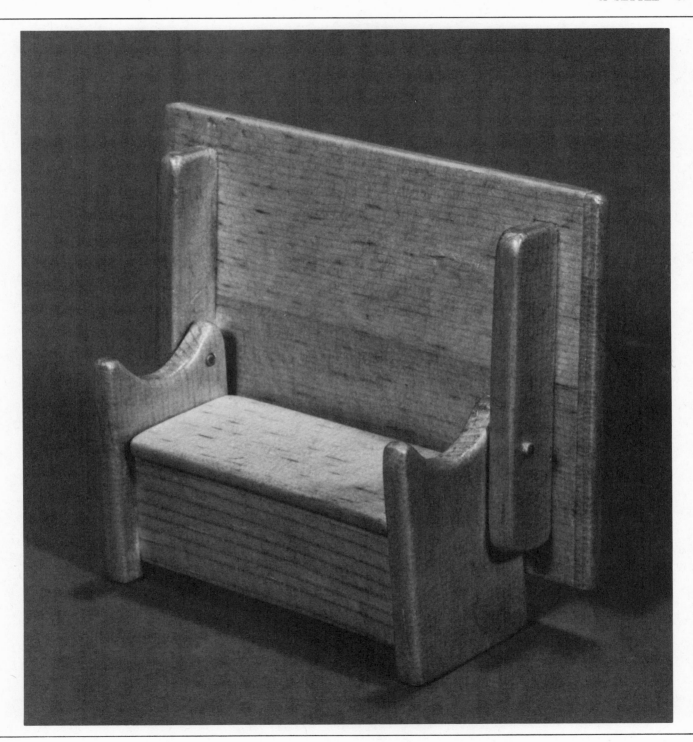

AN EARLY AMERICAN CHEST

Homemade chests were the first storage places for clothing and household linens in the early colonial period. Many of these old chests were made of pine and decorated by their builders in various ways. Some of the popular designs made on the front of the crude chests were diamond-shaped and heart-shaped. Others put their initials and the date on their handiwork.

Materials

2 pc $\frac{1}{8}$" x $1\frac{1}{4}$" x $1\frac{3}{4}$"—ends
1 pc $\frac{1}{8}$" x $1\frac{1}{4}$" x $2\frac{3}{4}$"—bottom
2 pc $\frac{1}{16}$" x $1\frac{1}{4}$" x 3"—sides
1 pc $\frac{1}{16}$" x $1\frac{1}{2}$" x $3\frac{1}{8}$"—A $\Big\}$ lid
1 pc $\frac{1}{16}$" x $1\frac{1}{4}$" x $2\frac{3}{4}$"—B

Construction

1. Using the diagram as a guide, prepare the end sections. The curved line can be made by using a five-cent piece to draw around.

2. If the front side is to be decorated, it is best to do so before attaching the sides to the ends. Outline the design on wood with a pencil and punch shallow holes with a small nail or large pin.

3. Glue the bottom between the ends $\frac{1}{2}$" up from the lower edge of the end pieces, and fasten the sides to the ends and bottom.

4. Make the lid by centering the B piece on the A piece. The A piece will extend $\frac{3}{16}$" at each end and $\frac{1}{8}$" at each side.

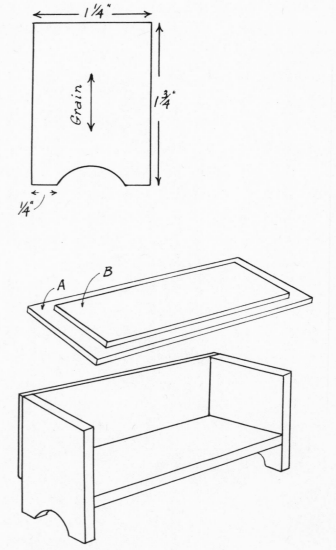

BEDSTEADS IN COLONIAL AMERICA

In colonial America a bedstead consisted of a frame strung with rope on which was placed a mattress filled with corn husks, leaves, or straw. As feathers became available, they were used as filling to make a featherbed. Many of the bedsteads had no footboard and a low headboard. Some frames were hinged to allow them to be folded against the wall in order to conserve space when not in use.

As the colonists and their descendants became more prosperous, four-posted bedsteads became more common. The posts were often connected at the top by a frame called a tester. The tester was covered with fabric, and many had curtains so that the bedstead could be entirely enclosed. On a cold winter night in New England, the drawn curtains helped to keep the occupants warm.

The trundle bed was designed to fit underneath the large bedstead. At night it was pulled out and used by the smaller children.

Another was known as the bundling bed, which was similar to any other bedstead except that there was sometimes a board running lengthwise between the headboard and footboard. The practice of bundling, or courting in bed, was common in the Old World and, as with many other customs, was brought to America by the immigrants. In earlier times it was condoned due to conditions that then existed. The houses were small, and young people could have more privacy while reclining in bed. It also saved firewood, and although wood was plentiful, it did have to be cut. One Connecticut clergyman once stated, "Bundling has prevailed one hundred sixty years in New England." He also said, "It is certainly innocent, virtuous and prudent,

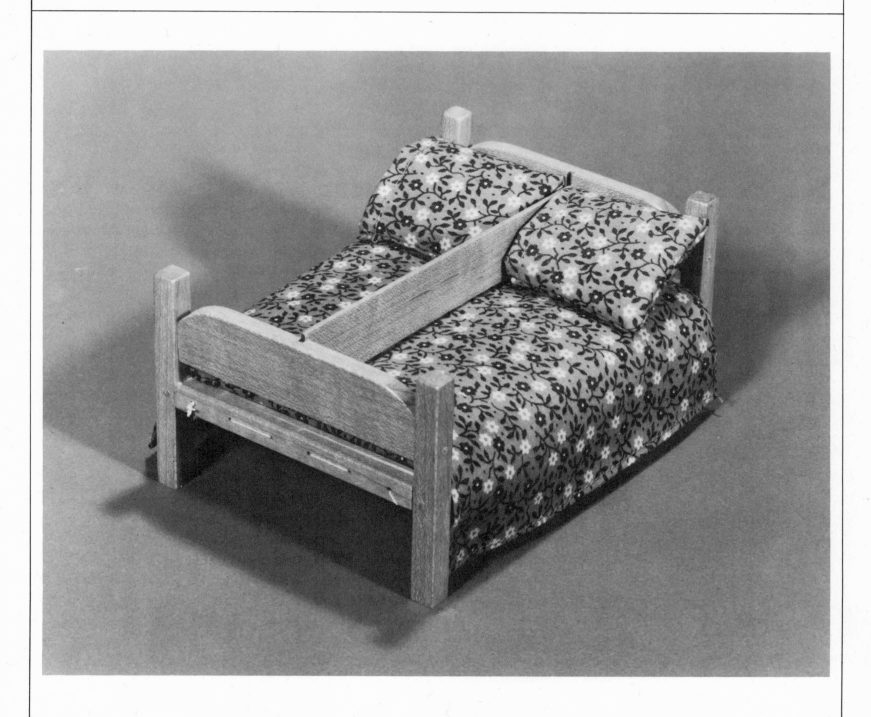

or the Puritans would not have permitted it to prevail among their offspring." Bundling, however, was not confined to New England and appears to have been common in many other parts of the New World.

A BUNDLING BED

Materials

2 pc ¼″ x ¼″ x 4½″—side rails
2 pc ¼″ x ¼″ x 3″—end rails
4 pc ¼″ x ¼″ x 2½″—posts
2 pc ³⁄₁₆″ x ¾″ x 3″—headboard, footboard
1 pc ¹⁄₁₆″ x ½″ x 4¾″—divider board
String for roping the bed

Construction

1. Drill no. 60 holes in the side and end rails. The first hole is ¼″ in from the end of the rail and the holes are ½″ apart.

2. Draw a light line on one side of each post 1″ from the lower end.

3. Shape the headboard and footboard as in the drawings, or leave them straight. With a file make a shallow groove down through the center of each board for the divider.

4. Using the lines drawn on the posts as guides, glue the end rails to the posts 1″ up from the lower end. Glue the headboard and footboard between the posts ¼″ above the rails.

5. Glue the side rails to one end assembly, and when the glue has set, glue the other end assembly to the side rails.

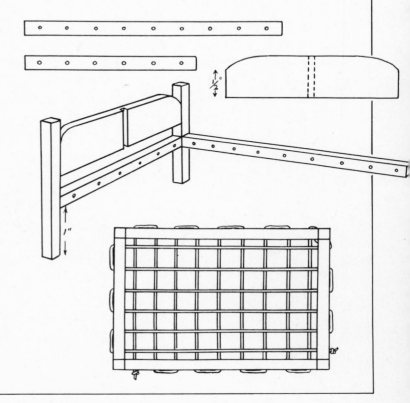

6. The old beds had rope strung back and forth between the rails to support the mattress. Beginning at the foot of the bed, tie a knot in the end of the "rope" being used to cord the bed. Make the knot large enough so that it cannot be pulled through the hole. Insert the rope through the corner hole in the rail at the foot of the bed. Carry it lengthwise of the bed through the opposite hole in the head rail. Then go on to the next hole in the head rail, back to the foot rail, and so on. When all of the lengthwise ropes have been put in, pass the rope inside one post and underneath the rail. Thread it through the first hole of the side rail and proceed as before. When completed, tie the end of the rope to keep it taut.

7. Press the divider board into the grooves.

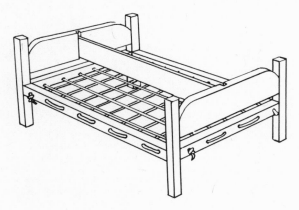

A TESTER BED

Materials

2 pc ¼″ x ¼″ x 4½″—side rails
2 pc ¼″ x ¼″ x 3″—end rails
4 pc ¼″ x ¼″ x 5″—posts
1 pc ³⁄₁₆″ x 1½″ x 3″—headboard
2 pc ¹⁄₁₆″ x ¼″ x 5″
5 pc ¹⁄₁₆″ x ¼″ x 3½″ } tester frame

Construction

1. Drill no. 60 holes in the side and end rails. Start the first hole ¼″ in from one end and space the holes ½″ apart.

2. Draw a light line on one side of each post 1¼″ from the lower end. Using these lines as guides, glue the end rails to the posts. The upper surface of the rails will be 1½″ above the floor.

3. Glue the side rails to one end assembly.

4. When the glue has set, glue the other end assembly to the side rails.

5. Make the headboard and glue in place between the posts ¼″ above the end rail.

6. Assemble the tester frame by gluing the longer pieces to the upper ends of the posts and then gluing the crosspieces to them.

7. Directions for roping are the same as for the Bundling Bed. (See page 75.)

8. Make the covering for the canopy by cutting a piece of material about 4¾″ wide and 5¾″ long. Place it over the frame, creasing the material along the edges.

9. For a curtain to cover the head of the bed and to extend about 2½″ along each side, cut a piece of material about 5½″ by 16½″. Hem the edges. Gather the top edge

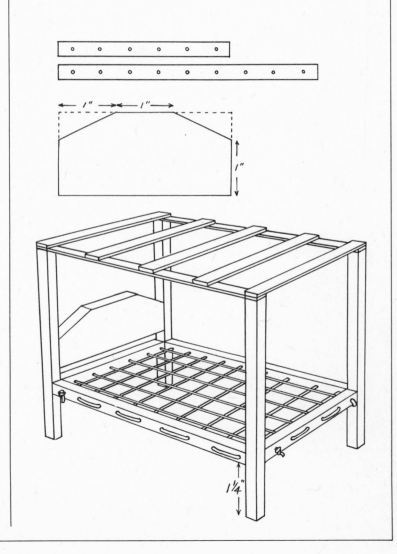

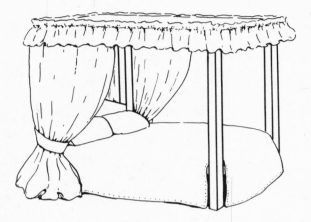

and sew it to the canopy covering. Use narrow strips of hemmed material for tiebacks to go around headposts and through an opening made in the curtain near the posts.

10. Cut a piece of material 1½″ wide and about 1¼ yards long for the valance to go around the upper edge of the canopy frame. Hem and gather and sew to the covering around the top edge of the frame.

11. Cut a piece of material 4¾″ wide and 6½″ long for the mattress. Fold material in half lengthwise, with right sides inside and edges together. Sew along one end and side. Turn right side out and fill with cotton or other material. Fold in the open end and sew together. Make the pillows the same way with two pieces of material 1¼″ wide by 1½″ long.

12. Make the covering for the bed from a piece of material about 6½″ wide and 7½″ long. Make cuts to fit around footposts and hem edges.

A TRUNDLE BED

Materials

    2 pc ¼″ x ¼″ x 3½″—side rails
    2 pc ¼″ x ¼″ x 2″—end rails
    4 pc ¼″ x ¼″ x 1″—posts
    2 pc ³⁄₁₆″ x ⅜″ x 2″—footboard and headboard

Construction

1. Drill seven holes in each side rail and four holes in each end rail with a no. 60 drill. Start the first hole ¼″ in from one end and space the holes ½″ apart.

2. Draw a light line on one side of each end post ¼″ from one end. Glue the end rails to the posts, using these lines as guides.

3. Glue the side rails to one end assembly, and when the glue has set, glue the other end assembly to the side rails.

4. Glue the head and footboards in between the posts.

5. Directions for roping are the same as for the Bundling Bed. (See page 75.)

6. Make the mattress for the trundle bed from material 2¼″ wide by 3⅝″ long. See directions for the Tester Bed (page 76).

7. Use a piece of material 1¼″ wide by 1½″ long for the pillow, and a piece 3¾″ wide by 4¼″ long for the covering.

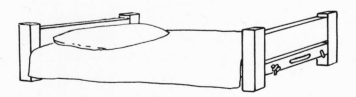

A PINE CUPBOARD

One piece of furniture often found in the seventeenth century home was a cupboard. There were many different styles, but they were all designed for the storage of dishes, tableware, pewter, and the like. In America, cupboards were often made from pine. Other woods used were chestnut, oak, poplar, and walnut.

Materials

2 pc $\frac{1}{8}$″ x $\frac{1}{2}$″ x $3\frac{1}{2}$″ ⎫
2 pc $\frac{1}{8}$″ x $\frac{1}{2}$″ x $1\frac{1}{2}$″ ⎬ ends

1 pc $\frac{1}{8}$″ x $\frac{3}{4}$″ x $2\frac{3}{4}$″—A ⎫
1 pc $\frac{1}{16}$″ x $\frac{1}{2}$″ x $2\frac{1}{2}$″—B ⎬ top

1 pc $\frac{1}{8}$″ x $1\frac{1}{8}$″ x $2\frac{3}{4}$″—C ⎫
1 pc $\frac{1}{16}$″ x 1″ x $2\frac{1}{2}$″—D ⎬ bottom

1 pc $\frac{1}{16}$″ x $2\frac{3}{4}$″ x $3\frac{3}{4}$″—back

1 pc $\frac{1}{8}$″ x $\frac{5}{8}$″ x $2\frac{3}{4}$″—E ⎫
1 pc $\frac{1}{8}$″ x $\frac{1}{2}$″ x $2\frac{1}{2}$″—F ⎬ counter top
1 pc $\frac{1}{16}$″ x 1″ x $2\frac{1}{2}$″—G ⎭

2 pc $\frac{1}{16}$″ x $\frac{1}{2}$″ x $2\frac{1}{2}$″—upper shelves

1 pc $\frac{1}{16}$″ x $\frac{7}{8}$″ x $2\frac{1}{2}$″—bottom shelf

2 pc $\frac{3}{32}$″ x $\frac{7}{8}$″ x $1\frac{1}{2}$″—front, lower part

1 pc $\frac{3}{32}$″ x 1″ x $1\frac{3}{8}$″—door

2 pc $\frac{1}{16}$″ x $\frac{3}{32}$″ x 1″—door hangers

1 paper clip or pin for hinges

1 pc round toothpick—for doorknob

Construction

1. Glue the shorter end pieces to one edge of the longer pieces. See the diagram.

2. Round off the front corners of the A piece and glue the B piece to it even with the back edge and ⅛″ in from the ends of A.

3. Fasten the D piece to the C piece so that the back edges are even and it is in ⅛″ from the ends of C.

4. Make the counter top by gluing the F piece to one edge of the E piece, allowing the E piece to extend ⅛″ at each end. Complete the counter top by gluing the G piece to one side of the other two and even with the back edge and ends of the F piece.

5. Draw light lines on the inside of the end sections ⅝″, 1¼″, and 2¾″ down from the upper end to locate the position of the shelves.

6. Assemble the cupboard by gluing the ends to the top and bottom and then putting on the back.

7. Install the shelves.

8. Put on the two front pieces, leaving an opening 1″ wide in the center for the door.

9. Drill holes in each door hanger ¹⁄₁₆″ in from one end. Also drill holes in the upper and lower ends of the door ¹⁄₁₆″ in from one edge and ⅛″ in depth.

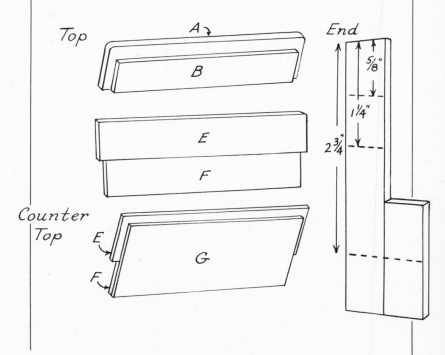

10. Glue one hanger to the bottom, between the two front pieces in the opening left for the door, with the hole to the right as you face the cupboard and against the front edge of the D piece.

11. Set the counter top temporarily in place and glue the upper hanger to the underside of the counter top against the edge of the G piece, with the hole in line with the hole in the lower hanger.

12. Drill a hole in the door about ⅜″ down from the upper end for the toothpick doorknob.

13. Insert a piece of wire or pin about ³⁄₁₆″ long in the lower hole and set the door on it. Also insert a piece of wire or pin in the hole made in the upper end of the door. Set the counter top in place with the hole in the upper door hanger over the wire. It will no doubt be necessary to round off the edges of the door on the side of the hinges. After the door is fitted satisfactorily, glue the counter top in place.

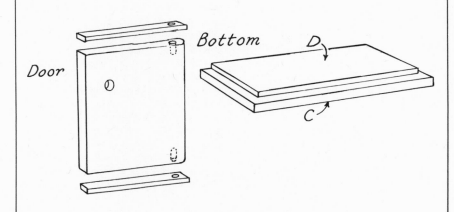

OUTSIDE THE HOUSE

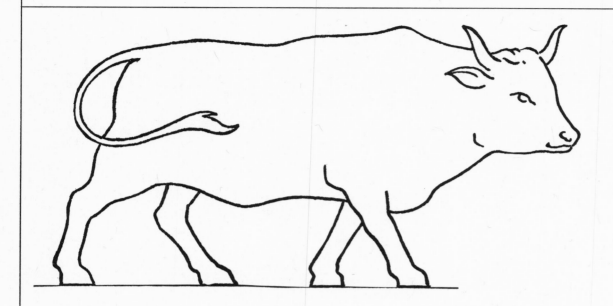

DIAGRAMS FOR HORSE AND OX

Trace the drawing, transfer outline to soft wood about ½″ in thickness and saw out. Round off the edges with a file and sandpaper or work down to shape with a sharp knife.

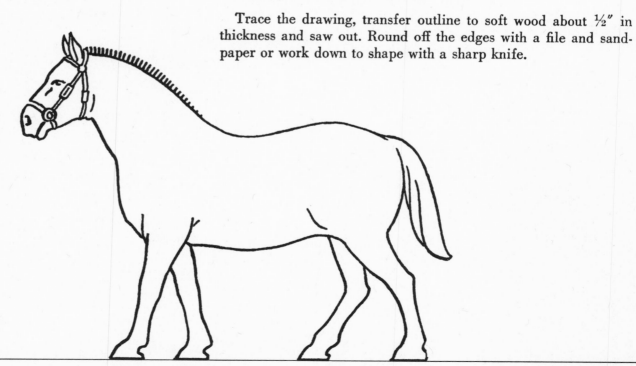

AN EARLY SLEIGH

In early colonial days, when there were few vehicles with wheels and the roads were little more than trails, people in the northern colonies did most of their traveling during the winter. Then the roads were made smooth and firm by a deep blanket of snow, and streams and rivers became solid highways of ice so that travel in sleighs was comparatively easy. It was then that the articles produced on the farm during the year were hauled to market and it was also the time for visits to the homes of friends, as there was less work to be done on the farms. There were many types of sleighs in use during the seventeenth and eighteenth centuries in America, and long caravans of them, loaded with farm produce, could be seen wending their way along the frozen highways of New England and the middle colonies on their way to the town or city. One common type was known as the Dutch sleigh. The people of New England called a sleigh drawn by two horses a pung and a one-horse sleigh a pod.

Materials

2 pc ¹⁄₁₆″ x 1″ x 6″—sides ⎤
2 pc ⅛″ x 1″ x 2⅛″—ends   ⎬ box
1 pc ¹⁄₁₆″ x 2½″ x 6¼″—bottom ⎦
3 pc ³⁄₁₆″ x ½″ x 2¾″—cross braces
2 pc ³⁄₁₆″ x 1″ x 7½″—for runners
1 pc ¼″ dowel 2⅛″ long—draw bar
1 pc ⅛″ dowel 5½″ long—tongue
   18 gauge wire for tongue brace

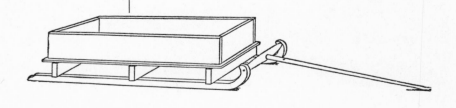

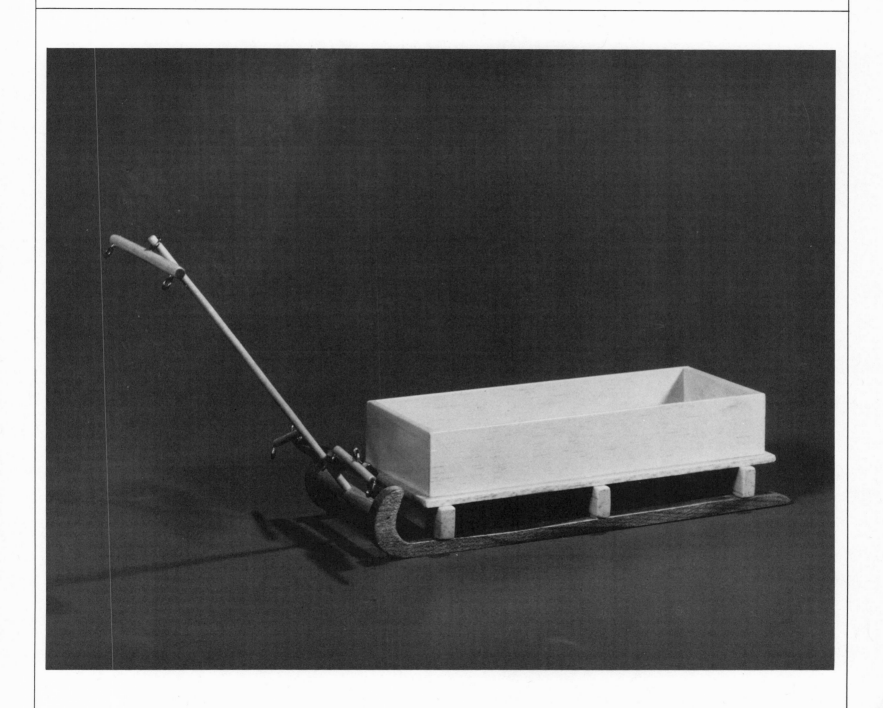

Construction

1. Trace pattern for runners on the wood and saw them out. Drill no. 60 holes in the curved end of each runner ¼″ down from the top. Peg or glue the three cross braces to the runners.

2. Make the box and glue it to the cross braces.

3. Drill a no. 60 hole ¼″ in depth in the center of each end of the draw bar. Taper the tongue as shown in the diagram and insert it in an ⅛″ hole drilled through the draw bar. Drill a no. 60 hole in the tongue ¾″ from the rear end for the pin to fasten the double trees to the tongue. Fasten the draw bar and tongue assembly in place with toothpick pegs. Make a set of double trees and a neck yoke.

ACTUAL SIZE OF END

3. DRAWBAR AND TONGUE

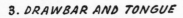

2 ⅛″

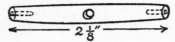

¾″   5 ½″

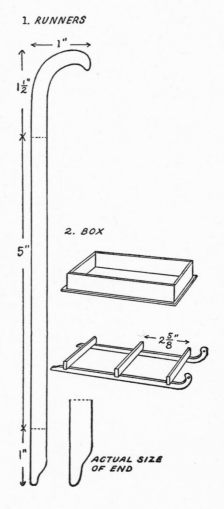

1. RUNNERS

1″

1 ½″

5″

1″

2. BOX

2 ⅝″

ACTUAL SIZE OF END

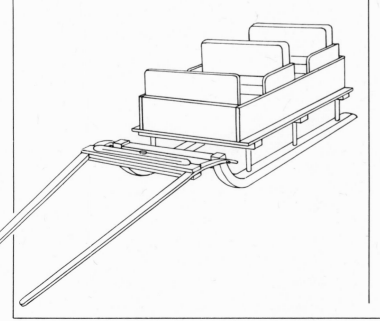

A DUTCH SLEIGH

Materials

2 pc $\frac{3}{16}$″ x $\frac{3}{4}$″ x 2″—ends ⎫
2 pc $\frac{1}{16}$″ x $\frac{3}{4}$″ x 4″—sides ⎬ box
1 pc $\frac{1}{16}$″ x $2\frac{1}{2}$″ x 4″—bottom ⎭
1 pc $\frac{1}{16}$″ x $\frac{3}{4}$″ x $2\frac{1}{8}$″—dashboard
2 pc $\frac{1}{16}$″ x $\frac{1}{4}$″ x $1\frac{3}{8}$″—dashboard holders
2 pc $\frac{1}{8}$″ x $\frac{1}{4}$″ x $3\frac{9}{16}$″—seat supports
2 pc $\frac{1}{4}$″ x 1″ x 2″—seat backs, A
2 pc $\frac{1}{4}$″ x $\frac{3}{4}$″ x 2″—seat, B
4 pc $\frac{1}{16}$″ x $\frac{1}{2}$″ x 1″—seat sides, C
2 pc $\frac{1}{4}$″ x 1″ x 5″—for runners
6 pc $\frac{1}{8}$″ dowel 1″ long
3 pc $\frac{1}{4}$″ x $\frac{1}{8}$″ x $2\frac{1}{2}$″—box supports or cross braces
1 pc $\frac{1}{4}$″ x $\frac{1}{4}$″ x $1\frac{7}{8}$″—crosspiece between runners
2 pc $\frac{1}{16}$″ x $\frac{1}{8}$″ x 5″—shafts
1 pc $\frac{1}{16}$″ x $\frac{1}{4}$″ x $2\frac{1}{4}$″—A ⎫
2 pc $\frac{1}{16}$″ x $\frac{1}{4}$″ x $2\frac{1}{2}$″—B ⎬ shaft crossbar
1 pc $\frac{1}{8}$″ x $\frac{1}{8}$″ x 2″ long—singletree

Construction

1. Make the box by gluing the sides to the ends. Then glue the bottom board to the sides and ends. The bottom will extend about $\frac{3}{16}$″ on either side.

2. Glue the dashboard holders against the inside of the front end. Set the dashboard on the front end, and glue it to the two holders.

3. Glue a seat support to the inside of the box $\frac{1}{16}$″ down from the upper edge of each side.

4. Make the seats by gluing piece B to piece A. Be sure that the seats fit in between the sides of the box. Glue on the sides $\frac{1}{16}$″ up from the underside of the seat board.

When set in place, the sides will rest on the upper edges of the box. Glue the back seat in place against the back end of the box and the front seat about ⅝″ in front of it.

5. Saw out the runners, using the diagram as a guide.

6. Drill three ⅛″ holes in each runner as shown. Also drill the hole at the curved end with a no. 60 drill.

7. Drive a piece of dowel into each of the ⅛″ holes in the runners.

8. Drill a ⅛″ hole in each box support ¼″ in from each end. Attach the runners to the box supports.

9. Center the crosspiece between the curved ends of the runners and between the holes drilled in the runners. Glue in place.

10. Soak the shafts in water and bend to the shape shown. Drill a no. 60 hole in each shaft ¼″ from the curved end.

11. Make the shaft crossbar by gluing piece A in between the two B pieces, which will extend ⅛″ beyond piece A at each end.

12. Drill a small hole for a pin or toothpick in the center of the singletree and the crossbar.

13. Attach the shafts to the runners with pieces of pins inserted through the holes in the shafts and into the crossbar between the runners.

14. Glue the shaft crossbar between the shafts and about 1″ from the back or curved end of the shafts. A rubber band will hold the shafts in the desired position until the glue sets.

15. Shape the singletree and fasten it to the shaft crossbar with a toothpick or a piece cut from a pin.

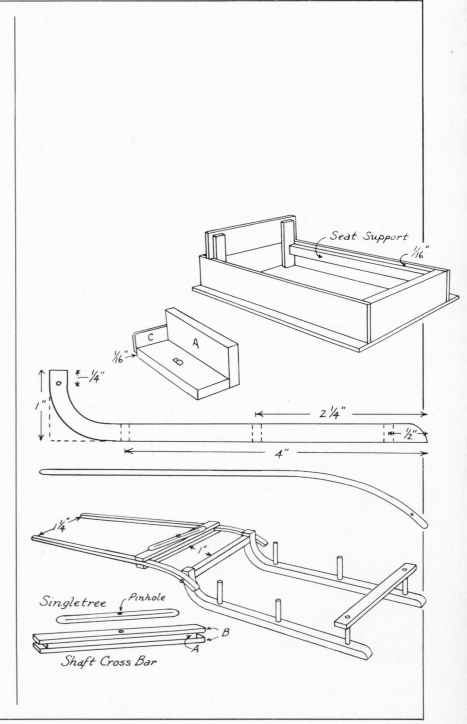

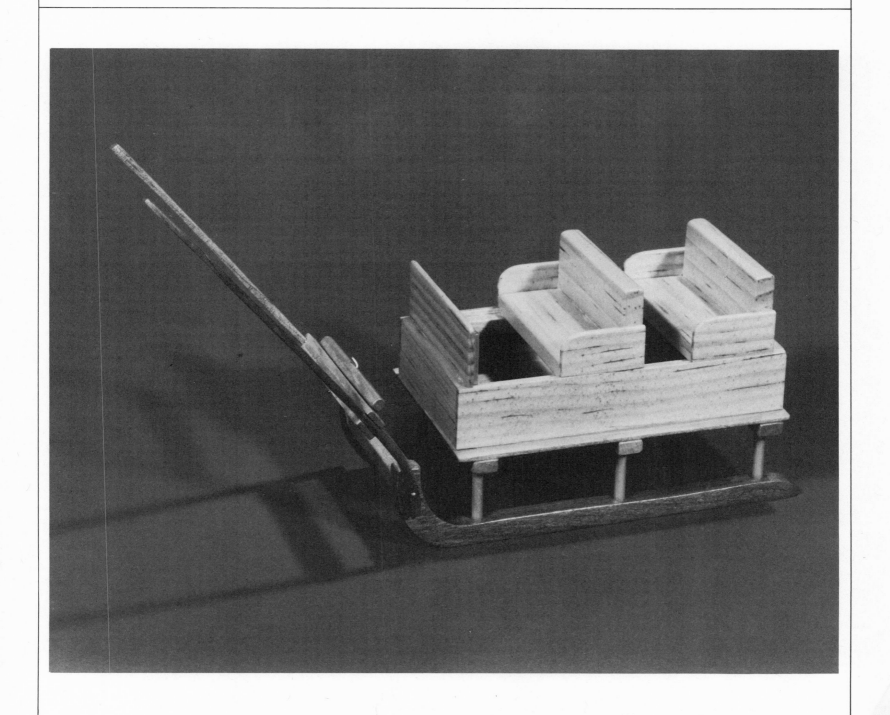

A CONESTOGA WAGON

The chime of the bells fastened above the necks of the horses and the rumble of the sturdy wheels of the Conestoga wagons were familiar sounds along the highways of America during the last part of the eighteenth and the first half of the nineteenth century. Thousands of these brightly painted freight carriers moved slowly along the roads drawn by sleek, powerful horses which were driven by a teamster with a whip under his arm and a "stogie" in his mouth. It is believed that the first of these wagons was built in the Conestoga Valley in Pennsylvania and received its name from the valley. These picturesque and distinctively American vehicles, with their curved bottoms and white canvas covers, were invariably painted red and blue and could carry five or six tons of freight. They played an important part in the history of America, helping to link our great country together at a time when there were no other means of long distance transportation. During the Revolution they were used to carry supplies to the American forces, and later to carry the settler and his family to the new lands of the West.

Materials

2 pc ⅛″ x 2″ x 9½″—sides ⎤
1 pc 3/16″ x 1¾″ x 2½″—front end ⎪
1 pc 3/16″ x 2″ x 2½″—back end   ⎬ box
1 pc 1/32″ x 2⅜″ x 8¾″—bottom ⎦

2 pc ⅛″ x ⅛″ x 9½″—A ⎤
2 pc ⅛″ x ⅛″ x 9″—B   ⎬ sides ⎤
14 pc 1/16″ x 1/16″ x 1⅞″—C ⎦   ⎪
2 pc ⅛″ x ⅛″ x 3″—A ⎤   ⎬ strips to strengthen box
2 pc ⅛″ x ⅛″ x 2⅝″—B   ⎬ ends   ⎪
8 pc 1/16″ x 1/16″ x 1¾″—C ⎦   ⎦

1 pc ¼″ x ⅝″ x 5″—axle ⎤
1 pc ¼″x ¼″ x 2½″ sand board ⎪
1 pc ¼″ x ⅜″ x 2¾″—bolster   ⎬ front axle assembly
2 pc applicator 1″ long—bolster stakes ⎪
1 straight pin ⎦

1 pc ¼″ x ¾″ x 5″ ⎤
1 pc ⅛″ x ¼″ x 2½″   ⎬ rear axle assembly
1 pc ⅛″ x ¼″ x 2¾″—bolster ⎪
2 pc applicator 1″ long—bolster stakes ⎦

1 pc ¼″ x ¼″ x 7½″—tongue ⎤
2 pc 3/16″ x 1″ x 4½″—tongue holders ⎬ tongue assembly
1 pc 1/16″ x ⅛″ x 2¾″—fifth wheel ⎦

1 pc 3/16″ x ¼″ x 7″—reach
2 pc ⅛″ x 1″ x 4″—reach braces
9 pc no. 2 reed about 9″ long—bows (Or broom straws or pieces
    of wood 1/32″ x ⅛″ x 9″)

2 pc 1/16″ x ½″ x ¾″—ends ⎤
2 pc 1/16″ x ½″ x 2⅛″—sides ⎬ feed box
1 pc ⅛″ x ½″ x 2″—bottom ⎦

1 pc ½″ x 1″ x ⅞″—tool box
2 12 spoke wheels 2¾″ in diameter with ⅝″ hubs 1″ long
2 12 spoke wheels 3¼″ in diameter with ⅝″ hubs 1″ long
    20 gauge wire for staples

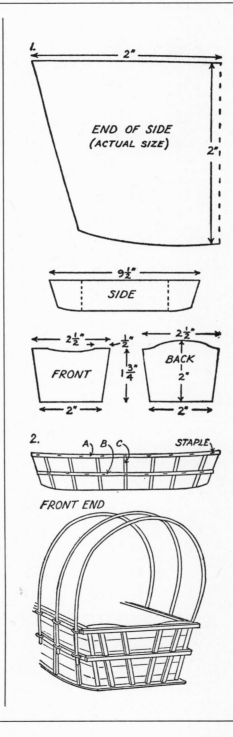

END OF SIDE (ACTUAL SIZE)

2"

2"

9½"

SIDE

2½"   ½"   2½"

FRONT   1¾"   BACK   2"

2"   2"

2.   A B C   STAPLE

FRONT END

Construction

1. Draw a line across one board, from which the side is to be made, 2″ from each end. Then trace the drawing on a piece of paper and cut out the pattern. Place the pattern on the board so that the straight end of the pattern coincides with the line drawn across the board and the upper edge coincides with the edge of the board. Make the other end in the same way. When one side is cut out use that as a pattern for the other side. Hold the two sides together in the vise and sandpaper them so that they are exactly alike. With sandpaper make the upper and lower edges slightly curved as shown. Cut out the two end sections. Make lines or grooves with an awl lengthwise on the sides and ends about ⅜″ apart to represent the boards. Glue or peg the sides to the ends.

2. Glue the A pieces along each side flush with the top edges of the box. Glue seven of the C pieces along the sides of the box about 1¼″ apart. Fasten piece B lengthwise through the center of each side. File out notches in B so that it will fit over the C pieces. Put the reinforcing strips on the two ends in the same way.

Allow endpieces A and B to extend over the ends of the sidepieces A and B. Cut off the lower ends of the C pieces so that they are even with the lower edges of the box. Make 36 wire staples, 18 for each side, and insert them into the A and B pieces about 1″ apart. Glue the bottom on. Hold with rubber bands until set. Put in the bows. If reed is used, flatten it by squeezing it between the jaws of the vise.

3. Make the front and rear axle assemblies as shown in the drawings. Round off the ends of the axles so that they are a little less than ⅛″ in diameter. Make notches in the axles for the tongue and reach braces. Drill no. 52 holes ⅛″ in from each end of the bolsters for the stakes, which should be tapered at the lower end.

4. Saw out the reach braces. Peg the braces to the reach about 3¾″ from the rear end. Set the ends of the reach and the braces into the notches cut out of the rear axle. Peg the bolsters to the axle.

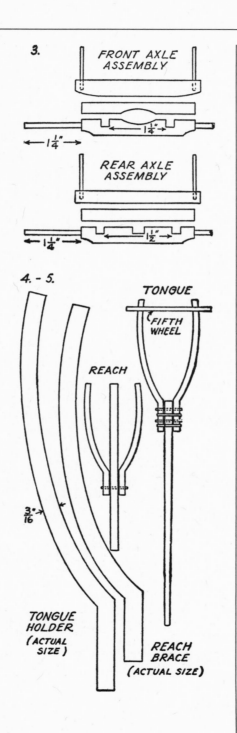

3. FRONT AXLE ASSEMBLY

REAR AXLE ASSEMBLY

4. - 5. TONGUE

FIFTH WHEEL

REACH

TONGUE HOLDER (ACTUAL SIZE)

REACH BRACE (ACTUAL SIZE)

6.

END OF FEED BOX

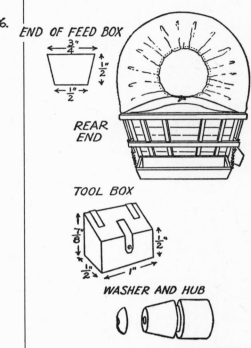

REAR
END

TOOL BOX

WASHER AND HUB

5. Make the tongue holders and peg them to the tongue. Make two bands from flattened wire and put around the tongue and holders. Put the holders through the notches cut in the front axle. The back end of the tongue should be about 1" in front of the axle. Fasten the fifth wheel to the ends of the tongue holders. Peg the sand board to the axle. Set the front end of the reach in the notch made in the center of the front axle, with the fifth wheel beneath the reach. Drill a pin-hole down through the bolster, sand board, reach and axle for a pin upon which the front axle will pivot.

6. Make the wheels. Drill ⅛" holes through the hubs and hold them on the axles with wooden washers or ⅜" buttonmolds. Make the tool box and glue it to the right side. Fasten the ends of the feed box to the ends of the bottom piece. Glue on the sides. Glue the box to the rear end or hang it with pieces of small chain. Make a neck yoke and whipple trees for the wagon. Make the cover from a piece of unbleached muslin about 9" wide and 12" long. Hem the sides and ends. Run a string through the end hems and tighten over bows. Fasten edges to staples with thread.